JOYFUL RECOLLECTIONS OF TRAUMA

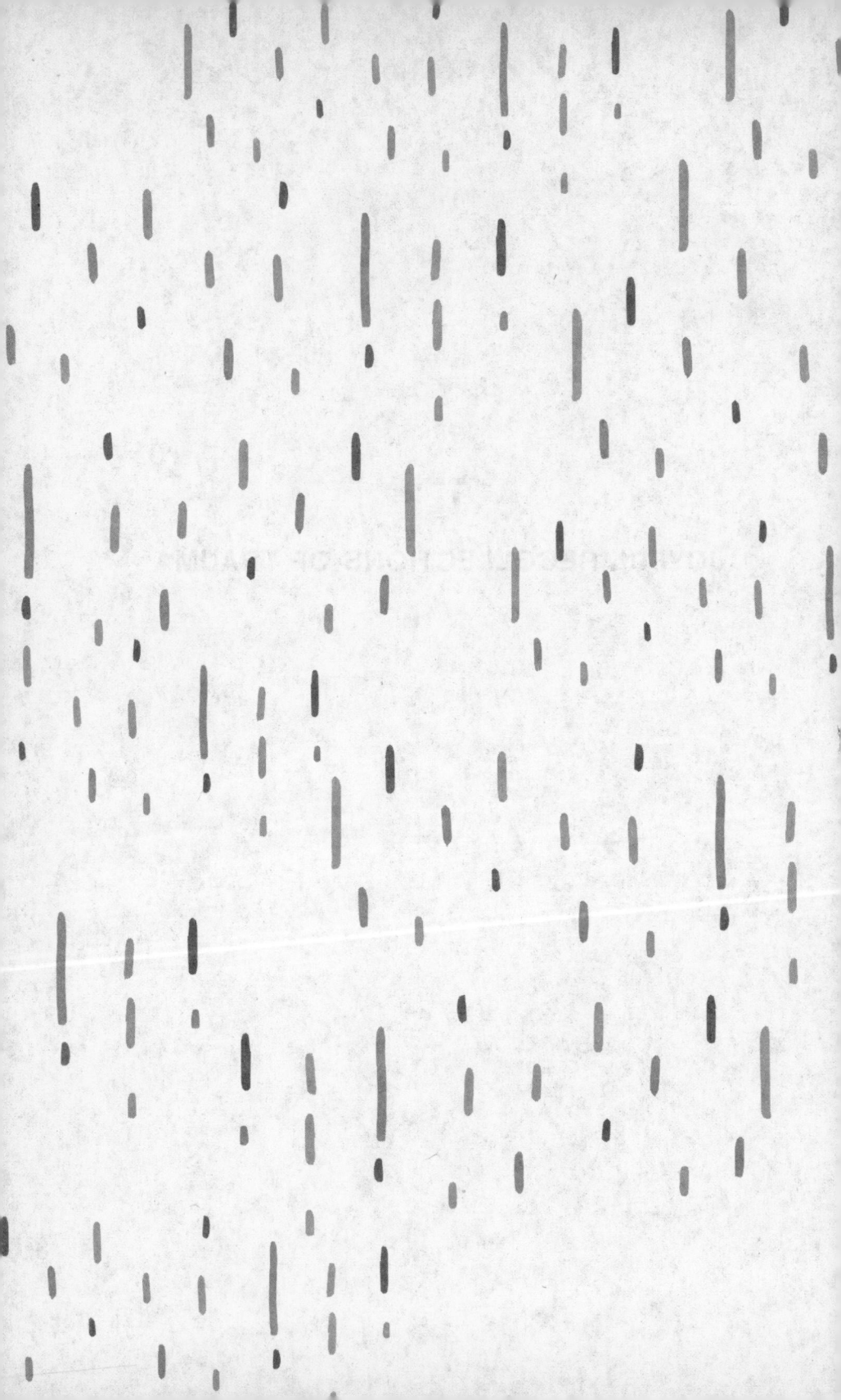

PAUL SCHEER

J☀YFUL RECOLLECTIONS OF TRAUMA

HarperOne
An Imprint of HarperCollinsPublishers

HarperCollins books may be purchased for educational, business, or sales promotional use. For information, please email the Special Markets Department at SPsales@harpercollins.com.

FIRST EDITION

Illustrations by anna1195/Shutterstock, Inc.; Beskova Ekaterina/Shutterstock, Inc.; yugoro/Shutterstock, Inc.; and Anya PL/Shutterstock, Inc.

Library of Congress Cataloging-in-Publication Data has been applied for.

ISBN 978-0-06-329371-7

24 25 26 27 28 LBC 7 6 5 4 3

To my parents, who made me who I am, and to June,
Gus, and Sam, who make me better than I was.

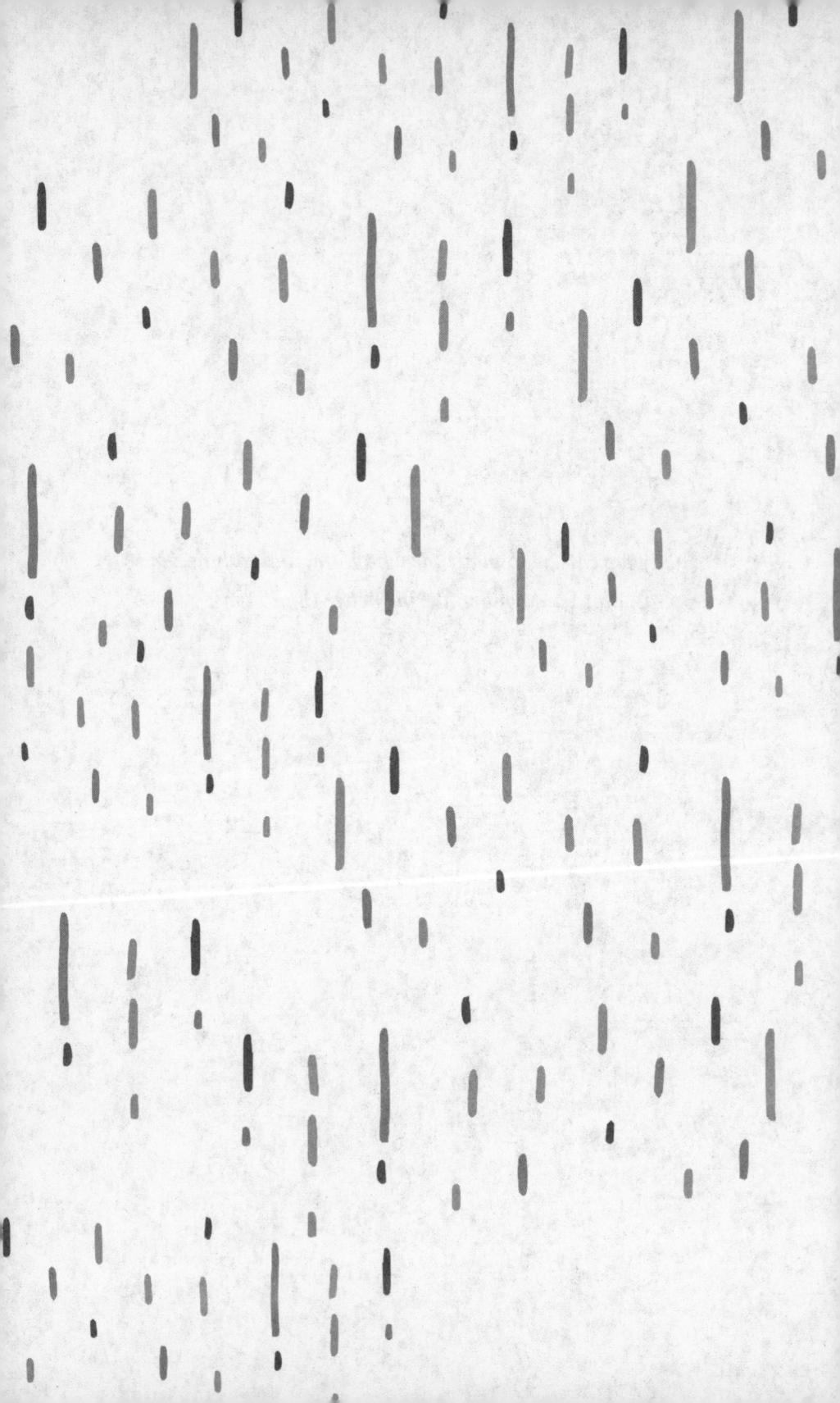

CONTENTS

CONTENTS

A NOTE FROM PAUL

The following is all true; while some names have been changed to protect me and others, the events and experiences detailed herein have been faithfully rendered to the best of my ability as I have remembered them. But also know that I'm not Marilu Henner; I don't have a photographic memory to recall the exact details of each day, and honestly, that seems to be a bit of a burden.

INTRODUCTION
THE COLLECTOR

I like to collect things. I started when I was a kid, with *Star Wars* action figures all neatly placed in my Darth Vader carrying case, their accessories in a side compartment so they wouldn't get lost. Then, it grew: cassette tapes (also with the proper portable carrying case), comic books (bagged and boarded), Garbage Pail Kids and NBA Hoops basketball cards (neatly organized in binders with plastic sleeves), movie souvenir cups from fast-food restaurants (if you could collect them all, I did), and VHS tapes, CDs, laser discs, and DVDs (always alphabetized and displayed for all to see). In addition to these store-bought items, I found myself collecting mementos from meaningful moments in my life: a stack of rubber-banded, faded, and ripped movie theater tickets; matchbooks from hotels and restaurants; notes passed in class; birthday and report cards; journals filled with detailed recollections of movies I had seen (so I wouldn't forget them). No matter where I go or what I do, I collect a little piece of the experience and preserve it.

As a child, I'd prominently display these objects around my bedroom. If I had put a velvet rope on stanchions in front of my door, you would have felt like you were in one of those historical homes that let you see back into the past, which was actually the present. I had inadvertently created a Smithsonian exhibit of me. I guess if I were smarter, like Sherlock Holmes, these mementos would all be in my mental palace, but what fun is that? I gotta show off my stuff.

Now, as I grow older, my bookcases and dresser tops are less crowded, but that instinct to collect stays strong. Whenever I have something I want to remember, a memento goes in a small, clear Sterilite six-quart stackable latching container. When one is full, I store it in the garage and buy another. These boxes, which have traveled with me from dorm rooms to apartments and houses like precious heirlooms, are filled with things that bring out so many different emotions. I laugh touching the playbill for Martin Lawrence's You So Crazy Tour, thinking about how my dad got us last-minute tickets to see my favorite comedian at the time (we assumed the material would be like his TV show but quickly realized we were in for a very different night when Martin opened talking about how many girls wanted to fuck him and how many girls he was fucking; I learned a lot that night). I cringe just looking at a journal I wrote while going through a breakup, which is so raw and embarrassing that I avert my eyes at the sight of the cover.

As I've grown older, I've also spent time going through the belongings of people I loved after they passed, finding their "boxes" (which, frankly, are not as well organized as mine). While I might not really understand exactly what I'm looking at, I know that the items were important to these people, and I pocket an item or two to put into one of my own boxes because it makes me feel closer to them. I know that kinda sounds like grave robbing, but give me the benefit of the doubt on this one. Sometimes I hope that my kids and grandkids, when they are older, might go through my boxes to learn about me.

But the thing is, will a string of Mardi Gras beads mean anything to anyone but me? Nothing is labeled. No one will know that I got the beads during an insane melee that happened post–Super Bowl in a small New Orleans bar after Channing Tatum got "served" by another patron in the bar and then the two of them did an impromptu dance-off. I didn't even realize that dance battles happened in the real world (clearly, I didn't go to musical theater school). For me, as a huge *Step Up* fan, watching Channing and his challenger was like watching *Step Up 3D* in actual 3D and with smells (good smells, but smells nonetheless).

Sometimes it feels like I'm essentially re-creating the ending of *Raiders of the Lost Ark*—boxes and boxes organized and stored, each full of stories but with no one to tell them. I clearly want people to know me. What's holding me back from telling these stories? Over the course of the past decade, some anecdotes about my childhood have come out in articles, podcasts, and talk shows, and the response frequently is "You should write a book." But I've always hesitated, because I knew that if I was going to, I'd

3

need to tell the *full* story—something I wasn't sure I was ready for. You want a funny anecdote, I have it. But really exposing the truth behind those anecdotes is something I'm anxious about doing. These are stories that only a handful of people actually know. So for the first time, I'm opening my boxes up and putting my collection of stories on display for all to see. I think some of them might surprise you as much as they surprised me.

Part 1

THE OLD TESTAMENT

I FOUND A FIRE

Confession: I'm an arsonist.

I guess, technically, I was more of a firestarter, kind of like Drew Barrymore in *Firestarter*, but with a way less convoluted backstory.

When I was in the fifth grade, I almost accidentally burned a family resort to the ground, just because I didn't want to ride a horse—but let's not get ahead of ourselves.

I was the only child of divorced parents, and when I was seven years old, my mom got remarried, to my stepdad, Hunter. He was completely different from my dad. He was twice divorced with multiple kids, a commercial truck driver for a local supermarket chain who wore cowboy boots, raised quail, and owned horses and guns. Lots and lots of guns. While not physically imposing, he carried himself with the energy of a person who was looking for a fight or just got finished with one. The knife on his cowboy belt only reinforced the image that this was someone you didn't want to fuck with. The first time I felt that energy directed at me was when I told him I didn't want to call him Dad but would prefer to call him by his name, Hunter. This was largely because my real dad was very much a part of my daily life, and honestly it felt weird to be told to call this other man, whom I barely knew, Dad. However, instead of accepting my decision with grace—he was already a father to his own kids, after all—Hunter stormed out of the room in anger and then proceeded to not speak to me and to ignore my presence like I was a ghost. I lasted about a week; I finally broke when he locked me out of the house in my pajamas and wouldn't let me in from the freezing cold until I said, "*Dad*, let me in." When I finally did, the door opened, and that was when I began to learn the delicate dance I needed to do around Hunter. I had to play by his rules to get what I needed.

At times, he could be gregarious, silly, and loving—then, as quickly as you could snap your fingers, he could become vindictive, mean, and violent. Once, during a game of Monopoly that he'd been losing, he landed on one of my properties. I looked down at my deed to see how much I was owed, but he locked eyes with me. "Do you really want to charge me?"

It was an odd question. Of course I wanted to charge him, that was the game. "*Yes!*" I laughed as I pointed to the rent owed.

But he gave me another warning: "Think about what you're doing."

All of a sudden, the energy shifted. Something much bigger was happening, but I didn't get it. As he held eye contact with me, I proudly told him that the rent was $375. Within an instant, he reached across the table, grabbed my neck, and started choking me. "I said, do you want to charge me!?"

I shook my head, gasping for air. "No."

He released me. I fell back to my seat, struggling to breathe, while he grabbed the dice and rolled for his next turn. That was it. We were back in the game.

Moments like this came as quickly as they went in our house. They were never acknowledged, never apologized for, and never seemed to have consequences, making me wonder whether they had even happened at all.

Hunter's three children from his previous marriages—Jennifer, Krista, and Hunter Jr.—came in and out of our lives. Hunter Jr. was an adult, and I didn't meet him until he moved in next door a few years after my mom married Hunter. Jennifer and Krista were teenagers who lived with their mother and would occasionally spend some of their weekends at my mom's house when I was at my dad's. Then, one day Jennifer moved in, for reasons never fully explained. All of a sudden, I went from being an only child to having a big sister, and she was cool. She always sported very heavy purple eyeliner, she loved the Who and Led Zeppelin, she had a boyfriend, and she wore a jean jacket with patches and buttons I didn't understand (but as a collector myself, I appreciated it). But our age difference was large: she was in high school, and I was only in the fourth grade. Since I spent my weekends with my dad, we wound up being weekday siblings, and our time together was limited. She didn't take the bus to school with me, her door was often closed, and she came home from work after I was asleep, but whenever we had time together, it was great. We'd talk about our crushes, go on walks, and during the holidays we'd sneak around the house to find hidden Christmas gifts.

Jennifer and I did go on two "family" vacations together. We once visited the Trapp Family Lodge, which I assumed was where *The Sound of Music* took place. (I only found out years later that the von Trapps weren't from Vermont and Hitler never made his way up the Eastern Seaboard of the United States.) Usually the places we visited were geared toward adults, and the kids were funneled off to their own activities. But the vacation we took to the Rocking Horse Ranch when I was in fourth grade was billed as a perfect merger of both experiences.

Rocking Horse Ranch in Highland, New York, was a "dude ranch"—a place where city slickers went to get out of their urban lives, like a family-themed Club Med. Rocking Horse Ranch offered a wide variety of horse-related activities: you could go horseback riding, watch a horseshoeing demonstration, take a barn tour to see the horses in their "natural" habitat, or play a game of horseshoes with comically large inflatable horseshoes. This place was a goddamn nightmare. I don't have anything against horses, but at the time, my family home on Long Island had a barn with three horses in our backyard, so vacationing where the number one attraction was horseback riding didn't really seem like a vacation. Now you might be thinking, *Paul, you had three horses; you can't just gloss over that—were you rich?* And the answer is no! I honestly don't know where they came from. I was told our family friend gave us first dibs on horses that were about to be put down, but as I type that, it feels like total horseshit (pun intended). I was a kid; I didn't ask too many questions. I just accepted the reality I was given—which, you will see, is a recurring theme in this book. I also never asked why, on a residential block, it was okay to corral the horses in our front yard and house them in a makeshift barn in the backyard at night. It feels like that should have broken a lot of zoning laws. But more on that in a bit.

When my family arrived at Rocking Horse Ranch, we were shown to two adjoining cabins that shared a porch—one for Jennifer and me and the other for Hunter and my mom. This was early on in their relationship, and it seemed like things were going well. It was a "honeymoon period," and I remember being grossed out by the amount of PDA they engaged in. I think part of the fun of a family-inclusive resort for parents is that they can drop off their kids at some activity, knowing they can't escape the property line, and the adults can then "get it on," which is exactly what I think my mom and Hunter were there to do. As a matter of fact, I don't want to think too much about that. Let's just move on.

I was excited that Jennifer and I would be spending all our time together, something I was really longing for.

In addition to horseback riding, each day at the ranch was packed with physically demanding kid-friendly activities: climbing, archery, swimming. I know that sounds like a dream to most people, but I wasn't super athletic. I was a kid who found reasons to opt out of gym class, and now I was forced to participate in a twelve-hour gym class that spanned multiple days. Since I was younger, I *had* to do the activities, and the only one I wanted to do, archery, I couldn't participate in because I wasn't old enough. Jennifer, on the other hand, was older and given the choice to do whatever she wanted, which was escape into the woods with her Walkman®, listening to bootleg Pete Townshend concerts and smoking cigarettes. But here I was, plopped into a group of kids I didn't know, doing things I could do but didn't like to do at home.

After the first two days, I begged my mom and Hunter not to make me participate in another day of leisurely horse rides and awkward snack breaks. We made a deal: I could skip out of the mandatory "fun" activities as long as I didn't bother the adults *all day*—until 5:00 p.m.! I think they were trying to call my bluff. But I took the challenge with reckless abandon.

As the sun rose the next morning, a smile crossed my face. I had nothing to do. The world was my oyster, as long as I didn't leave the property. As an only child, I was used to keeping myself occupied for hours on end. Making a snack became a cooking show for no one. I never did chores; instead I became a character hired to do my chores and would boss myself around. I talked a lot to people who weren't there and also to myself—anything to break up the silence of being all alone in my house. When I did just play, I'd improvise movies of my own creation and act out all the characters. Since I was a kid who grew up on action movies—the ones with troubled cops whose personal lives were a complete mess and who had multiple vices but were damn good at their jobs—I created my own, Lance Hanson, a disgraced cop in his mid-forties: every kid's dream. Lance was always being called back to the force for one more case. Whenever I was alone, the movie would start right from where it had ended the last time I played.

That first free day on the ranch, I was back to being Lance, on a big case. To outside observers, it probably just looked like I was wandering aimlessly around talking to myself, which I was. Little did they know that the three-foot-wide dry creek bed behind our cabin was going to be the scene of an epic battle. In my mind it was the East River, and Lance was trying to stop a mad bomber (Is there any other kind?) from blowing up the Roosevelt Island tram. As I tried to talk down the bomber (also played by me), I leaped back and forth across the ravine in a heated war of words, but talking wasn't working. This bomber had one thing on his mind: carnage! Lance was having a hard time in his personal life; he'd started smoking again. Luckily, I knew where Jennifer had hidden her stash. I grabbed a cigarette from the pack hidden behind her bed, plus a pack of Rocking Horse Ranch matches from the room's ashtray; I love a prop.

I put the cigarette in my mouth and lit it. (I know it sounds like I was smoking, but I swear it was for the part.) I puffed on my cigarette and the scene began.

EXT. Roosevelt Island Tram—Night
Kasmarek and Hanson stand across from each other on top of the tram.

Kasmarek
(vaguely European accent)
Well, if it isn't Lance Hanson. I thought they put you out to pasture for killing all those kids.

Lance
It wasn't my fault! That bus had no brakes.

Kasmarek
Funny, neither does this tram. It's an express . . . to hell.

                    Lance
You can't do this!

                    Kasmarek
How do you say, yes, I can!

The scene needed more tension, so I decided to rachet up the
drama.

                 Female Voice
Lance? Is that you?

                    Lance
Diane?

                 Boy's Voice
Daddy?!

That's right, Lance's ex-wife, Diane, and child were on the tram,
and I played all four roles simultaneously.

                    Lance
                 (to Kasmarek)
You sonofabitch.

  Lance's Ex-Wife   Son
    Lance! Help us.   Daddy! Help us.

Kasmarek

I wish I had a camera. I love family
reunions.

Lance
(to his ex-wife and child)
Diane, just calm down.

Kasmarek

She left you because you weren't around,
and now she'll die because you are. How
poetic.

Lance

I have a poem for you. Roses are
red. Violets are blue. If you blow
up me, I blow up . . . *You!*

Lance throws his cigarette at Kasmarek. He
catches on fire and falls off the tram.

I was so into the scene, writhing around in pain as Kasmarek,
that I didn't realize that I had thrown a lit cigarette into a patch of
brush.

Kasmarek

No! No! How ironic! I light the
fuse but now I am the fuse.

I continued the scene and mimed climbing down into the tram and reuniting with my ex-wife and my son.

                    Son
    Daddy!

                   Lance
                 (to Son)
    Let's go get some ice cream.

                   Diane
    I love you, Lance.

They passionately kiss.

(Note: I acted out this kiss and it was sexy.)

Happy with my performances, I moved on to do something else only to see that a small fire had started where the cigarette had landed, and was spreading, quickly.

I tried to stomp it out—which didn't work. I'd never really seen anything like this before. My heart started racing. I stared as the flames grew. I would have said "Fuck!" at this moment, but it was a rating issue; I always wanted to make my fantasy movies PG so kids like me could see them.

Back to the fire—I didn't know what to do. I knew all about stop, drop, and roll, but that's only good when *you* are on fire. No one ever tells you how to put a fire out. So I did the only thing I could think of: I ran inside the cabin to get . . . a cup of water.

When I reached the room, Jennifer was back, sitting on the bed. I was out of breath and freaked out, but when I saw her, I tried to act calm.

"What's up?" I asked.

"Um, nothing," she responded. "What did you do today?"

"Nothing. Just walked around."

"Wanna watch MTV with me?" she asked.

"Sure, but first, I'm, uh, just thirsty. I'm going to get some water."

I ran to the bathroom and grabbed a cup—a cup that was so small it was more like a thimble. But I filled it with water and ran back outside, where the fire was spreading. Every second it was getting closer to the cabin. But no worries, I was going to put a stop to it! I threw my dollop of water onto the fiery blaze.

Nothing happened. I needed a new plan, but unfortunately I didn't have one. So I ran back inside, past a fire alarm I could have easily pulled, to get more water. When I reentered the room, I tried to act casual as Jennifer intently watched MTV.

"Do you like this song?" she asked.

"Is that the song from *Family Ties*?"

"Mike and the Mechanics."

"No, Billy Vera."

"I think it's Mike and the Mechanics."

As we debated, I suddenly remembered—*water*!

"I'm thirsty!" I said again, grabbing two glasses this time and running outside.

By the time I returned to the blaze, the fire had spread to the

cabin's back wall. I tossed the two cups of water into the blaze—
and still *nothing*! Now I was in a full-on panic.

But if something doesn't work twice, it will definitely work a
third time . . . So I went back inside to the bathroom sink. But this
time, Jennifer stopped me.

Noticing my red face and very heavy breathing, she knew that
something was up. "What are you doing?"

As she rose to ask the question, she stood directly in front of the
back cabin window, where the flames now had risen so much that
they silhouetted her body.

I pointed outside. She turned, and I watched the look of shock
register on her face.

I shouted, "There's a fire, and I didn't start it!" (That is definitely
what an innocent person would have said.)

We ran outside to find the blaze creeping up the back wall of the
cabin. We stood there, frozen, too young to know how to deal with
this. I blurted out again, "I didn't do it! I just found it."

"Go get your mom," Jennifer said. I didn't move, just repeated
my alibi. This time she yelled: "*Get help!!*"

I started to run—and then froze. I looked at my watch, then at
Jennifer. "But it's not *five o'clock!*"

"*Who cares?!*" she roared as she ran back into our cabin to get
more water.

I ran to my mom's room and banged on the door; no one answered. I banged again. Still no answer. I kept furiously knocking
until, through the door, I heard "Yes?" It was my mom's voice,
but she sounded weird—different. I didn't really take that in, just
shouted, "*The cabin is on fire!*"

Mom opened the door. She was in a bathrobe, and there was caviar and a bottle of champagne on the bed behind her. Clearly I was interrupting some afternoon delight. Again, I don't want to think about this.

Seeing me standing there, her face fell. "*What?!*"

"I found a fire, and it won't go out!"

"I found a fire" seemed to be the best tactic. It put me in a heroic position, making me essentially a human Lassie. All I knew was that I couldn't go down for this. The punishment for this crime would be *huge*.

Mom and Hunter ran out in their bathrobes to witness the flames racing up the entire back wall and roof of the cabin. Smoke was billowing as other guests started to come out of their rooms. I'm sure most of them thought there was some sort of impromptu family s'mores event happening.

I kept broadcasting my lie to whoever would listen until a Rocking Horse Ranch representative rode up on horseback, of course. *Oh, they loved their horses.* He told us that they had called the fire department and we all needed to stand back. More and more people kept arriving on the scene to stare at this blaze I'd started.

"What happened?" someone asked. At that point, my hope was to fade away into the background of the chaos.

Then my mom announced, "He found it! He found a fire."

Jennifer nudged me and tried to pull me back into our room, but a Rocking Horse employee told me to wait—he had some questions.

Damn! I was the criminal and the witness. This was going to be tough. Thankfully I had a lot of experience playing two roles.

The fire truck appeared, and firefighters got to work hosing down the back of the cabin. The flames went out quickly; the damage appeared to be only cosmetic. The lead firefighter approached me and asked me to follow him. I walked about fifty feet away from my mom and Hunter. The firefighters sat me on their truck and circled me, blocking my view of everything past them. Luckily, I had conducted and been subjected to many interrogations as Lance and other assorted criminals, so I knew how to act, or so I thought. I stood tall, but being surrounded by a bunch of actually tall men firing questions at me really made me feel smaller than ever. I knew I *had* done all of this, and if they found out, I was going to jail.

As a child, the idea of going to jail was very real for me. In the short time I'd spent with Hunter, he had often attached the threat of jail to the smallest things: "If you don't hang up your coat, you'll go to jail." Or "If you don't wash your plate in the sink, you're going to jail." He said it so frequently, presenting it as an eventuality rather than a possibility, that I was convinced there was a jail for kids who misbehaved. But to make matters worse, Hunter didn't stop at telling me I would be going to jail; he would explain what would happen to me when I was there. He would describe how not only would I be locked away from my friends and family, but I would also be raped on a daily basis. Yes, raped. I didn't even know what sex was as an eight-year-old, let alone rape. My mind created these vivid pictures that weren't unlike rape, but at that age, the idea was even more horrifying, because I couldn't truly comprehend it. If I could go to jail for not picking up my coat, starting a fire was way worse; that definitely was a crime.

I was done for, moments away from going to jail and being raped for the rest of my life. I was scared, and so there was only one thing to do: keep *lying* and commit even harder to my lie.

The firefighters kept pressing about what I'd seen, and I kept repeating the same story: "I was wandering around out back, and I found a fire." I knew I needed to give them more. So I started suggesting ways it could have started.

"Maybe the sun was so bright it bounced off the windows, and it worked like a magnifying glass." *Hmm, no takers on that one.* Then I went with what I knew: "Or maybe someone threw a cigarette out here."

The cigarette theory caught the firefighters' interest, so I offered to look around the crime scene for any evidence I could find. I searched frantically until I found a piece of a cigarette filter right where the fire had started. "I found it," I said, running over to the firefighters. "Someone was smoking. They must have accidentally started the fire."

Notice I used "accidentally" because even though I was blaming a fictional person, I didn't want anyone to go to jail and get raped.

One of the firefighters approached me and asked, plainly, "Did you start this fire?"

The conviction in his voice sent me into momentary shock. I stumbled and bumbled. "No, what?! . . . I found it."

He looked at me again. "Empty your pockets."

I did, and I pulled out the matches from the hotel. He knew he had me. "Was it your cigarette? Were you smoking out here?"

I was insulted by the accusation. "No. I don't smoke." Little did he know the actual truth of why I had the cigarette was way more embarrassing.

He still didn't believe me. "Just tell us the truth. You don't want to have to leave early and go home, do you?"

I mean, the answer was "Yes! I do want to go home!" But I stood firm and told the biggest lie of the day: "No, I love it here. I swear I found it."

We stared at each other. I don't know if he bought it, but I wasn't going to change my story. I held firm. Then, from somewhere behind me, I heard Jennifer say, "He couldn't have started it. He was watching TV with me."

Instant alibi. I was saved! The firefighter knew he was deadlocked. He looked to the ground and shook his head as he whispered under his breath, "Just be careful." And he walked off.

Jennifer put her arm around me and gave me a big smile. My big sister had saved me! We never talked about what had actually happened or what was going through her mind in that moment as she stepped in and protected me. Decades later, as a parent of two sons who are often at each other's throats, I've noticed how, when stuff gets real, they have each other's back. As an only child, I didn't know how much I had craved that—the support and protection that comes from a sibling. And as my life at home with Hunter grew more and more fraught in the years that followed, this protection was something I really needed. Unfortunately, Jennifer stayed with us for only about nine months, but in that short period of time I had a sibling—one who saved me from being horribly raped in jail. For that, I'm forever grateful.

THE BOX

Early in my relationship with my wife, June, we were watching the movie *Cool Hand Luke*. If you haven't seen it, all you need to know for our purposes is that it's about a bunch of men on a prison chain gang under the thumb of an excessively cruel warden who, whenever they make the slightest mistake, sends them to spend a "night in the box"—a small, dark room with little air and hardly any space to move. After a night in the box, the men come out looking utterly destroyed. So when I said matter-of-factly, "It doesn't seem that bad," June grabbed the remote, paused the movie, and looked at me with concern in her eyes.

"*What?* You're joking, right?"

The moment hung in the air and I had a choice: I could lie or just double down. I doubled down. "I mean it kinda looks . . . peaceful."

June turned again, almost in slow motion, and looked at me like I was an alien. "*Peaceful??*"

"Yeah, I mean it's kinda relaxing," I said. "Can't go anywhere. Can't do anything. Just you and your thoughts."

"So you want to be tortured?"

"No!" I replied, "I mean, I'm not thinking about it that way—it just seems like a nice chance to take a break from the world."

June gave me a stare that I've come to know too well: she looks at me suspect—trying to determine whether or not I've been replaced by some sort of alien who is just wearing a Paul suit or I'm pranking her on a hidden-camera show (something I had to promise her in our wedding vows that I would never do). "This is too upsetting to me. I can't talk about this anymore," she said as she got up to leave the room.

In a last-ditch attempt to prove I was normal, I tossed out, "I'd make it nice! I'd bring crosswords and an iPad." It didn't help my case.

But this is nothing new. Ever since I was a kid, I've loved to hide. While some kids dreamed of walking into their closet and finding Narnia, I was happy to just go into my closet and be in darkness. Silence and space were my own magical land.

I think this fascination started with my childhood bed. It was on a platform, and underneath were two bookcases and two long drawers. I once noticed that the back wall of one of the bookcases was loose, so I started pushing on it until it completely detached. When the flimsy piece of cardboard hit the floor on the other side, I saw there was a whole world back there—I mean, technically it was just an empty space under my bed, but this was the biggest discovery of my young life. I had found a secret passage, a doorway to the unknown. I crawled through the bookcase shelf and into this new space. It became my kid cave, my after-hours club, my pied-à-terre. I spent hours there with books, flashlights, and a handful of toys. Then one day it was over—not because anyone told me I couldn't hang out there anymore, but because I had grown too big to fit through the bookcase hole. I was unceremoniously evicted from my own Narnia, due to the size of my hips. I didn't want to let this place go, so since that day I've continued trying to re-create the safety and solace of that space wherever I can.

While other kids' favorite games were baseball and soccer, mine was hide-and-seek. And I would *really* hide—like, a *What if zombies were out there trying to kill me?* level of hiding. If I could get under the floorboards, I would. This commitment always created issues with my friends, because I wouldn't come out until I was found. What started as a fun game often devolved into irritated friends begging me to stop and reveal myself, which then would lead to pissed-off parents having to join the search, all while I chilled out, silently having the time of my life behind a dresser or in the attic with a box over my body. I never got why everyone was so bent out of shape until I realized that they had been searching for the better part of an hour and the only person it was fun for was me. This was my sport and I was a pro at it, but little did I know my skill at hiding would almost cause an international incident.

Public schools in my neighborhood were rough: my friend's brother was stabbed through the hand with a pencil in third grade. So my parents enrolled me in this small private school on Long

Island that seemed to cater to wealthy European and Asian families who were in the country for short periods of time on business and, oddly, the rest of the students were local middle-class kids. So, when you were invited to a birthday party, you really never knew what you were going to get. Would it be a mobile petting zoo and bespoke cupcakes or pin the tail on the donkey and a sheet cake from the local supermarket? But I should have known something was up when my friend Elena's third-grade birthday invitation specified "formal attire." Elena's party was unlike any I had ever been to; she lived in a giant mansion on the water, and a large yacht was moored to the side of the house.

Here's what I didn't know: Elena's father was the bodyguard for ███████████, a pretty notorious dictator. But even though the dictator was in ██████████████████, Elena's family lived on Long Island. We had to get past an armed security checkpoint to get to her house, which was like a royal palace. A waiter told us to "follow the cake" to the main room. I didn't know a cake could leave the table but this one did. The cake was built like a staircase; part of it traveled down a tiered table the way a wedding dress train trails behind a bride, and we followed it into the main room.

The party was an all-out affair—bigger than I could have imagined—with clowns, magicians, balloon artists, and karaoke; the yacht had a dance floor! It was overwhelming. So instead of partaking in all the sanctioned activities, I suggested my favorite game, hide-and-seek. The rest of the kids jumped at it. Elena and I partnered up; she knew the house, and I knew dark places. We made the perfect team. We raced through the house, which felt like it went on for miles. She finally picked a bedroom that didn't have a bed. When I asked where the bed was, she informed me the room was a closet. *Wow!* We turned off the lights and lay down on two empty shelves, waiting for someone to find us. Occasionally, we thought we heard someone, but no one ever came. This was a perfect hiding spot.

It had been over an hour when we heard footsteps approach the door. We both tried not to laugh but giggled as we covered ourselves with towels. We heard a hand on the doorknob, which we had locked; they tried again, and *bam*! The door flew open with a kick, and a three-person tactical team burst in shining flashlights into the darkened room. I didn't even take in that the men who had found us were heavily armed; I was just bummed we were found. Apparently Elena's father thought she had been kidnapped rather than just playing a game of hide-and-seek with the best in the biz.

* * *

In my own very different home, hide-and-seek wasn't just a sport: it was a survival skill. As I mentioned earlier, when I was growing up, my home looked like a lazy kid's *Animal Crossing* island. Next to the house sat a barn with horses, a corral, quail pens, two dog runs, and a backyard aboveground pool. Plus there was always an odd assortment of trucks and trailers all around the property. I recently drove by my old house, a place I hadn't visited in decades, and was shocked to see not much had changed. As a matter of fact, the same broken bench that sat on the side of house for years was still there. This house had gone through multiple owners and our garbage was still on the lawn. Which might explain why when a friend saw a picture of my house, she said knowingly, "Oh, you grew up in a trailer park?" I explained I didn't, but it definitely had the vibe of one.

PAUL SCHEER

Growing up with a lot of animals in your backyard might seem fun and magical, but it was a lot of work. I had to muck the corrals (a nice way of saying I picked up shit), clean the dog run (another nice way of saying I picked up shit), sweep under the coop (yet another way of saying I picked up shit), and feed all the animals (which made them produce more shit). It was an endless cycle. I was in my own chain gang of one, and my warden, Hunter, was a very tough taskmaster, not unlike the one from *Cool Hand Luke*. When I disobeyed, there were consequences. Here he was the boss. I had no recourse, unlike in the house, where my mom could break it up. We often were left alone out there and I was treated like one of the animals. Most of my time in the barn was spent literally being pulled around by my hair, to "get my attention." Like a dog, my nose would be rubbed in whatever mistake I made. I was sprayed with hoses, locked in dog kennels, kicked, choked, and often left alone to tame animals three times my size. I don't mention these things cavalierly, but they were done with such regularity that they don't even register as the traumatic events they were.

When I was about nine, my chore list expanded to include bringing hay down from the loft. The top half of our barn was an unfinished loft, a dark, hot space where hay was stored. I loved watching the truck with a hay ladder load up the loft every few months, but I hated going up myself. There was only one way in: I had to climb up a thirty-foot steel ladder that led to a little hole in the loft's floor. The ladder was cemented into the ground, but because only one end was secured, it always had some give—not something you need or look for in a ladder. I've never been scared of heights, but I started to freak out the first time I went up to the loft. First of all, the ladder went up *really* high. The only thing stopping me from falling was me, and based on my lack of athleticism, a fall wasn't out of the question. I stopped about twenty feet up in a panic, not knowing whether I could finish the climb. Hunter, who was watching from below, goaded me on: "What are you waiting for?! You scared?"

"No!" I stammered. "I was just taking a break."

"Go faster, it won't be scary," he bellowed. So I took in a deep breath, and I raced up to the top of the ladder. Which put me in a more precarious situation because now I was even more scared and higher up.

When I got to the top, I realized that height wasn't going to be my only issue. Getting up into the loft would be almost impossible for someone my size because the ladder didn't quite reach the loft; it ended right below the hole in the loft's floor. It was the dumbest design flaw I've ever seen. If the ladder just extended two more feet, you could easily climb into the loft. But now I'd need to balance on the wobbly ladder with my feet while taking my hands completely off the ladder and reaching up into the loft using my elbows to an-chor me on either side of the hole. Then, in one swift motion, I'd have to do an elbow push-up to propel my body into the loft. The most accomplished yogi would have a hard time manipulating his body this way—and if I made a wrong move, I'd fall four stories onto a concrete floor. *I'm not doing this. I'm done.* So I made the choice to go back down. Once I was on the ground, I begged Hunter not to send me back up: "I'll do more chores, just not that one."

He laughed at me. "Stop being a such a girl. It's easy," he said, and he started climbing the ladder himself. He was much taller and wider than me, but when he reached the top, he too had a momentary struggle. He shimmied and shook and managed to pull himself up through the hole. He taunted me from above: "Come on, Paulina."

I tried again. As I reached up into the loft, I immediately felt unsteady, as if I were losing my balance. I clamped my hands back on the ladder and retreated to my safe position. I kept trying but never making any real progress. My sloppy attempts to climb through the hole only served to make Hunter laugh harder as he watched me from above. I could feel tears welling up in my eyes as I stood frozen by fear, and I tried desperately to hold them back. Suddenly, I felt Hunter's hand on the back of my shirt, and he yanked me up into the loft. I released the ladder and for a moment the only thing protecting me from a straight drop was his brute strength. My feet moved like Shaggy's in *Scooby-Doo*, trying to find the ground as he pulled me forward and tossed me on the floor. "See, that's how you do it!" Then, without missing a beat, he stepped over me, grabbed some hay bales, threw them through the hole down to the ground, and began to climb down the ladder. All the while I lay there on the floor, in shock, relieved that I had made it up but paralyzed with fear about how I was going to make it back down.

Going down seemed even more intimidating than getting up. I crawled to the edge and peered over, seeing the thirty-foot drop with brand-new eyes, and it was terrifying. There were two ways to get down. You'd have to just throw your legs over and walk down a straight ladder facing forward while sliding your hands down the ladder behind you (*nope*), or you'd have to get on your belly and let your feet slip over the edge, then feel around with your sneakers until you found a rung on the ladder and could start your descent. But because there was nothing to hold on to on the loft floor, you'd have to find ways to slow your belly shimmy before your foot and the rung made contact, because if you went too fast, you'd fall straight to the ground. I didn't know how to do that, especially on an un-sanded wood floor, so I did the next best thing. I called for help.

I yelled out, "I can't get down!" but no answer came. I screamed. No one responded. "*Help me!!!*"

Had Hunter left? Was he was just ignoring me, or was he hearing my screams and secretly laughing at me? I tried peeking my head out of the hole one more time to see whether I could spot him, but he was gone. Now here I was, in the dusty and hot hayloft, trapped, stranded—alone. Gnats buzzed around my face. It was silent, dark, and oddly peaceful. *Wait a second—I like this.* My heart rate began to go back to normal. I was free and safe from the world below, a world I couldn't normally escape. It may not have been intentional, but I was here now. A smile crept across my face. I was hiding.

I knew Hunter couldn't leave me up there forever, and I knew I wasn't getting down without help. It was a battle of who was going to cave first, but little did he know I could stay up here as long as I wanted. Up there in the hole, I was safe. I was in control and I could protect myself mentally and physically. I guess my mom fi-nally forced Hunter to help me down, and in that moment, I took great joy in watching him be contrite. I had won and now he had to escort me down the ladder. I had made him do something he didn't want to do. Finally, I had power. Just like Paul Newman in *Cool Hand Luke*, I might not have been able to beat the warden, but I could drive him crazy and that might be how I'd survive.

NO PHoTOS. NO PARENTS.

In the summer of 1988, my dad and I were visiting Los Angeles and had signed up for this service called Hollywood on Location. For seventy-five dollars the service would get you a listing of the locations of every TV and film production shooting in LA that day and what celebrities would be on set. Then you could drive to the location in the hope of seeing a scene being filmed or, better yet, meeting an actor or actress—which in retrospect seems really sketchy. But this was the 1980s. Stalkers be damned.

Hollywood on Location didn't guarantee you'd meet or even see any stars, but we were told there was a pretty good chance if you just waited around long enough. We had allotted one whole day for this adventure. We scanned the list of the productions and stars. Sadly, my top choices (Eddie Murphy, Steve Martin, Robin

Williams, and Michael J. Fox) weren't shooting anything in LA on that day, but there were a few names and shows we recognized. So we set out across Los Angeles to find us some celebrities. We zigzagged around the city, from Beverly Hills to Marina del Rey, to the Valley, back over the hill to Culver City, and eventually to downtown LA. The day was a huge success. I met Michael Landon, David Carradine, Gerald McRaney, Markie Post, and a guy who I thought was Kirk Cameron but who turned out to be the stunt coordinator for the Miami Vice Action Spectacular at Universal Studios, which was pretty cool, too. Every one of these stars went out of their way to sign an autograph or take a picture. For a huge fanboy, it was a dream come true.

Our last stop of the day was the set of a movie called *Communion*. I didn't want to go because it sounded like a religious movie, but it was on the way back to the hotel so we figured why not. Most of the sets we visited that day were EXTs (exterior locations), which meant the scene was outside and you could see the actors as they worked. It wasn't until we parked that we realized *Communion* was an INT (interior location). The Hollywood on Location team told us to always avoid INTs, because you could spot actors only when they were either headed to or coming from set, and you could waste hours standing around and never see anyone. Since we were already here, we figured we'd give it a shot. We hung around for about an hour and didn't see a thing; it appeared that we had struck out. As we were headed back to our car, a mustached security guard approached. "Here to see some movie stars?" he asked. We told him all about our amazing day and the people we were meeting;

he then pointed to a large building across the street and told us that inside this building was the biggest star of them all, Christopher Walken. The name didn't ring a bell until my dad reminded me Walken was the bad guy in *A View to a Kill*, at the time my favorite James Bond film. My eyes went wide. "I can meet Max Zorin?" The guard smiled: "You bet. Wait here." He crossed the street and entered the building. A few minutes passed, and when he returned, the security guard told us if I wanted to meet Mr. Walken, there were some rules. "Mr. Walken is working on a very secretive project and you can't bring your camera inside and also no parents." I'd have to go alone. I gave a look to my dad, who said, "Up to you?" I smiled, passed my camera to my dad, and followed the security guard across the street. He opened a door to a darkened warehouse.

The guard motioned for me to enter in front of him. I walked in alone as he closed the door behind me and waited outside; the only light in the entire room came from the crack where the door had been left slightly ajar. Then from the darkness emerged Christopher Walken. The sliver of light illuminated his face perfectly as his dour expression changed to a smile. He approached me and got down on a knee. "Hello, little man. I hear you like movies." I just nodded my head. He continued, "I like movies, too. We're making a movie right now about aliens. Real aliens. Do you believe in aliens?" I was so tongue-tied all I could do was nod my head yes.

"That's good," he responded as his smile grew bigger.

"The light hurts my eyes," he said, in an attempt I guess to explain why we were meeting in the dark. I wasn't a great conversationalist in these moments, so instead I held out my autograph book like he was a character at Disney World. Walken signed and then grabbed me by both arms, looked me right in the eyes, and said, "Don't let anyone tell you what you can and cannot be." He then patted me on the head and walked away back into darkness. Right on cue the security guard came in and escorted me back to my dad.

That might be one of the best experiences I've ever had meeting a celebrity. I firmly believe, however, that because of how wonderful that experience was, I am now forever cursed to have the most awkward experiences when meeting anyone I'm a fan of.

It started not long after this meeting with Walken, when I met Alan Alda. I was having lunch with my grandma and her bridge friends at a local spot near her house, and two tables over, Alda was holding court with a table of friends. Alan Alda was a big star, and while *M*A*S*H* wasn't my show, I appreciated the gravity of the sighting.

My grandma and her friends were giddy that there was a celebrity in their local spot. They all sat up a bit straighter, talked a little louder, and took more than a few furtive glances at his table. The restaurant was practically empty, so I'm sure Alda felt their attention. Grandma and her friends wanted to meet him, but they were too shy, so they pushed me to go over to his table instead.

I didn't want to. *M*A*S*H* was a TV show I tolerated, as a bridge show that got me to the reruns of the shows I really wanted to watch, like *Diff'rent Strokes* and *Benson*. If Robert Guillaume had been over there, I'd have been there in a second. But Grandma wouldn't let it go. She cajoled me, "You want to be an actor, right? Well, you have a once-in-a-lifetime opportunity to meet this *giant star*. What if he discovers you? You simply must go over there, or you will regret it forever." It was the same logic she used when she tried to have me get Susan Lucci's autograph when she was standing in line for communion (not the movie but the sacrament) when we saw her at my grandparents' church. Luckily, my grandfather put a stop to that, but he wasn't at lunch and she kept pressing for me to go over and meet Alan. I finally relented. I approached his table and stood awkwardly nearby, waiting for a break in the conversation. There was none. I stood for what felt like five minutes until one of Alda's friends gestured to me: "I think we have company, Alan."

"Mr. Alda, I'm a big fan, could I have your autograph?" I asked.

Without turning in my direction, he said, "No." It was as if he was swatting away a fly.

I was shocked. I hadn't met anyone who just said no! I started to walk away, and he called after me, pointing, "I bet you don't even know who I am."

"From *M*A*S*H*" were the only two words I could make come out of my mouth.

He beckoned me closer to his table and said, "Name two more things you've seen me in and I'll give you an autograph." So now I was standing at this table in front of Alan Alda and his lunch guests, all of whom were smiling and laughing at the unwinnable game going on. I was completely at a loss. "Um," I stammered. Alda cut me off: "Not such a big fan, huh?" He then just waved me away. I was crushed. If it wasn't enough to be humiliated in front of Alda and his friends, I walked back to my grandma's table and I saw them laughing hysterically at me and the rejection that had just occurred. Now I looked like the idiot for something I didn't even want to do in the first place. "I guess you aren't going to get discovered after all," one of my grandma's friends cackled.

It was the first time I was humiliated in front of a celebrity, but it wouldn't be the last. Just in case you missed it, in the literary world that is what we call foreshadowing.

KEVIN MCCALLISTER COULD NEVER . . .

Being Kevin McCallister in *Home Alone* is the ultimate kid fantasy. Not the new *Home Alone*, where there are no bad guys and everyone seems to be an asshole—I'm talking about the original where loving parents accidentally leave their child home alone as they race off to France for Christmas break. Then, as they are trying to get back home, the kid has to fight off burglars who, at a certain point, seem to be more intent on murdering him than robbing him. And then, everyone learns the true meaning of Christmas—which, if I'm reading it correctly, is "Always be nice to your creepy neighbor because you never know when you'll need him to break into your house with a shovel."

Watching this movie with my kids is an amazing experience. They get the wish fulfillment of being a kid and having the house to yourself, no parents, no rules—awesome. But they also experience a kid version of *Die Hard* in which an eight-year-old has to fend off adults double his size and intent on killing him, and wins. For a kid, to believe that's possible is a triumphant feeling. Kevin is a hero to kids everywhere! As someone who has fought a home intruder and escaped multiple weirdos trying to do me harm, Kevin McCallister has got nothing on me. However, he does have me beat when it comes to constructing Rube Goldberg devices. How did he find the time?

I spent one summer in a military school–themed summer camp, which was just as fun as it sounds. My parents became suspicious about what was going on in this camp when it seemed like we were doing manual labor disguised as "activities." The final straw, however, was when I told my parents that the counselors insisted on watching all the boys when they peed to avoid any "funny business" in the bathroom. Upon hearing this, they immediately pulled me from camp. While they might have been slow to action on dealing with issues inside the house, they were surprisingly quick to deal with outside threats. However, there was a month left of summer break, and none of the other camps were accepting new kids this late in the season. So I was offered the chance to stay home alone for a few weeks. Something I repeatedly asked for at the start of each summer. This was a dream come true.

I slept in, watched TV, ate cereal for lunch, made Shrinky Dinks, wore pajamas until after noon, read comics, made myself spicy virgin Bloody Marys (just V8 and Tabasco), and listened to Weird Al loudly on the family stereo—life was good. I didn't have a care in the world.

One morning, I awoke to a pounding at my front door. Most kids probably wouldn't be this scared about a knock on their front door.

But I had been on edge lately because just a few months earlier, there had been an incident when I rode my bike about a mile down the road to our town center to get a Slurpee at the new 7-Eleven. The 7-Eleven was a big deal for me. It felt like it put our little town on the map. I watched its construction with bated breath. Finally, I'd have access to Slurpees, Big Gulps, and even comic books. This was going to be my new hangout. So when my mom let me go to 7-Eleven by myself, I had a whole plan mapped out for my adventure. I'd get my Slurpee, then cross the street to wander around the aisles of the "fancy" video store for as long as I wanted, without anyone rushing me, and then when I found the movies I wanted, I would walk across the parking lot to the low-rent video store, which was where we had an account, and rent them. I never understood how these two video stores sustained their business directly across the street from each other in such a small town, but there seemed to be so much animosity between them that customers of one would never go to the other one. It was our Hatfields and McCoys. But without my parents around, I was free to make my own choices and didn't have to play by their rules.

As I rode my bike into the parking lot of the new 7-Eleven, I felt accomplished. There was a feeling of pride in going somewhere by yourself and arriving at your destination unscathed. But that feeling didn't last long, because as I put my bicycle into the bike stand, I heard one of the nicest things said in one of the scariest ways: "Nice bike!" I turned around and faced three burly men in camo pants, trucker hats, and T-shirts (which were the universal fashion choices of men in our neighborhood). They were drinking beer and sitting on the hood of what I assumed was the leader's truck. Now, while I knew not to talk to strangers, I also wanted to be polite, so I said, "Thanks," and quickly walked inside. I felt their eyes on me. As I wandered around the 7-Eleven, I kept peering out the window, checking on the men to see if they were still there. They were. As I filled my Slurpee cup, I noticed they had surrounded my bike. I was nervous. But at this point, nothing bad had actually happened that could be reported. What would I do, tell the 7-Eleven cashier that some guy said, "Nice bike!"? Also, this was a time when a kid reporting their gut feelings of stranger danger didn't really hold weight with most people. So I paid for my Slurpee and exited. As I did, the men who stood around my bike turned, looked me up and down, and silently parted, allowing me access to my bike. *Okay, maybe I was overreacting!*

Then Mr. Nice Bike asked, "Where did you get your bike?"

Again, I did the dance of not wanting to talk to strangers, but at the same time I knew ignoring them wouldn't work either, so I meekly said, "I got it for my birthday."

"Is that so?" the leader replied.

So far a transcript of this conversation would look like something out of *Mister Rogers' Neighborhood*, but it was all in the tone. After years of dealing with Hunter, I recognized this calm before the storm. As I bent down to unlock my bike, a glass beer bottle flew past my head and exploded on the bricks in front of me. I froze, staring at the glistening red brick as beer trickled to the ground. My heart raced. The leader approached.

"That's my son's bike! You stole my son's bike!"

Now while this was definitely not true, my heart was racing like a criminal caught in the act. I struggled to answer, tripping over every word, "No, no, this is my bike." But I'm sure I sounded as guilty as I was innocent.

He stood firm. "That's my son's bike. I want you to come back to my house and tell my son that you stole his bike and apologize."

While I was scared, this type of intimidation wasn't new to me. The only thing that was truly frightening was that it was three men and not just one. I knew exactly what to do: run. Which in retrospect made me look hella guilty (I've never used *hella* in a sentence before, but I think it works perfectly here).

I dropped my Slurpee and ran out of the 7-Eleven parking lot, across a busy two-lane roadway. Horns blasted at me, as I escaped . . . into a much bigger parking lot, with nowhere to hide. Was running the best plan? Probably not. Shouldn't I have just run back into the 7-Eleven? Absolutely. But too late for that.

Two of the burly men gave chase while Mr. Nice Bike jumped in his truck and followed behind. I quickly ran into the supermarket and hid. I was trying to act casual. I should have been yelling for help. But still I felt like I could solve this on my own. This tendency to take matters into my own hands developed after years of making calls to my mom at work and asking her to come home early to put out some fire between me and Hunter. Now, while her presence would always help, I also felt an added guilt because I had called her away from work. I knew it negatively affected her ability to make a living. So it became ingrained in me to not ask for help. Because asking for help in my mind was creating a problem. So I often put on this brave face, content to figure stuff out for myself—which now had me crouched in the produce aisle trying to avoid capture or worse.

I watched the door to the supermarket. I saw two of the burly dudes enter and start looking around, which was my cue to leave. I had seen enough cop movies to recognize this game of cat and mouse. I escaped the supermarket unseen, and then I was back in the parking lot where the leader sat idling his truck. I panicked, not knowing whether he saw me. I was blocked in and running out of options. So I ran into my last bastion of hope, the "fancy" video store. *Wow, this place is fancy.* I had never been in there and I couldn't believe what I was seeing. The store felt like it was from the future (by way of the '80s): everything had a silver sheen to it; there were mirrors, framed movie posters, a second floor, and a working popcorn machine. Suddenly I snapped to. *Wait a second, what are you doing? You aren't here to window-shop. You are being chased right now.* Maybe here, among my favorite things in the world, I felt safe enough to ask for help—which I did, loudly and from the entire store. I screamed, *"Help! Someone is chasing me and trying to steal my bike!"*

In a normal town, this would be the moment when the owner of the store might grab a bat from under the counter, put me in a safe place, and ask, "Who's doing this to you?" But instead, after I let out my pleading scream, I remember everyone turning, looking at me, and then promptly going back to work. No one did anything! I stood frozen, my hands still outstretched from my previous declaration, and I watched my plea fall on deaf ears. Was this because I wasn't a member of the store? This rivalry was no joke. Now that my last hope was dashed, I was going to have to deal with these men alone. I exited the store—again facing the truck. This time the leader saw me. My options were exhausted so I booked it home.

My house was about a mile away from the town center, and I ran as fast as I could, hearing the rev of the truck's engine getting closer as I raced home. I knew I couldn't outrun them so I scooted off the main road onto someone's front lawn, and then I jumped a fence and was able to disappear or at least go to a place where they couldn't follow by car.

I ran through backyards and down side streets until I arrived back at my house. I busted into the house and unraveled the entire story to my mom and Hunter. They sprang into action, and we headed back to the 7-Eleven.

When we arrived, a police car was in the parking lot, lights blaring. Cops were talking to a 7-Eleven employee on one side and Mr. Nice Bike on the other. I stayed in the car as my mom and Hunter approached. I felt like I was in the back seat for an eternity, watching everyone speaking but not hearing anything that they said. My bicycle was still there, too, locked to the rack like I'd left it. A cop finally approached our car. My parents opened the door, and the officer spoke to me gently, apologizing for what I had just gone through. He told me the 7-Eleven cashier had seen the bottle thrown, and the fancy video store owner had called the police, too. The cop explained that Mr. Nice Bike's son had a similar bike and he was just confused. So he wasn't a bad guy; he was just looking out for his son. The officer asked whether I would forgive the man or wanted to press charges. At this age, I didn't know what *pressing charges* meant. The officer explained that if I pressed charges, these men would be forced to go to court and maybe go to jail, so I instantly said, "*Yes!*" I wasn't really much of a social justice person as a child. But, the police officer continued, if I pressed charges, I'd have to put my home address on the form, and then that man and his friends would know where I lived. "So it's up to you . . ." the officer said. That ultimatum hung in the air like the smell of a 7-Eleven bacon-wrapped hot dog. Something was off.

In retrospect, I don't know how a minor could even press charges or what side this cop was working, but he worked me good. I said no. I didn't want these guys to know where I lived. Then they brought Mr. Nice Bike over to apologize, which he did. He even offered up a playdate with his son and suggested we could take turns riding my bike; though the offer sounded sincere, it also was something I'd never want to do. I unlocked my bike and we all left. My mom and Hunter followed behind me as I pedaled back home. Going out on my own had really lost its sheen.

* * *

Back to that frightening knock at my door. My immediate thought was *Oh my God, they found me—I don't know how, but they found me.* (At that time I was very much into *Back to the Future*.)

Now, I hadn't been given many rules from my folks for being home alone, but the main ones revolved around the door: "Don't answer the door." "Don't open the door!" Easy stuff. So I just waited for the knocking to stop. But it didn't, it kept continuing, and it got harder and louder. And then—silence.

I assumed the person had realized that no one was home and

left. But I wasn't taking any chances. I stealthily snuck up to the front window to see whether the coast was clear before I opened the door, and to my shock, there was a big-biceped beardo pacing in our driveway. I ducked down under the window to avoid him seeing me. My heart started to speed up.

He once again approached the porch and banged on the door, but this time he also started peering into our front windows. I sat frozen, crouched under the window, as he stared through the one right above me.

"*Hunter!*" he screamed. I felt relief hearing him yell out Hunter's name. At least now I knew it wasn't those bike guys coming back for me.

That relief was short-lived as he went back to the door and started banging so hard that a picture fell off the adjacent wall and shattered as it hit the ground. My first thought was *I'm so going to get blamed for that*, but before I could even deal with that fear, the doorknob started to turn, first gently then violently. Thankfully the door was locked. *Relief!* But what about the back door? *Panic!* The weirdo and I seemingly had the same thought at the same time, because I saw him move across my front yard, heading toward the back.

We had a sliding glass door at the back of the house that led to a covered outdoor patio, and neither door was ever locked. I knew I needed to get to both of them before he did. I bolted to the back of the house. I had to beat him to the door.

But I was too late. He entered the patio just as I flicked the lock on the sliding glass door's handle. I was now face-to-face with this man. He knew someone was home. We stared at each other, separated by this pane of glass, and I watched as his scowl turned into a smile that was even more scary than the scowl. He asked gently, "Is your daddy home?"

I shook my head no. He got closer to the glass and continued to press, "I know he's home, let me talk to him." Now, I knew I was never supposed to answer or open the door, but the biggest rule I was sworn to obey was the one I was about to break: when I looked him right in the eye and said, "No one is home. I'm here all by myself."

As a kid, I knew you're never supposed to tell anyone you are home alone. I knew I had just showed my hand, but I thought that maybe if I was honest with him, he would believe me and leave me alone. Being honest with him, however, had the exact opposite effect. You'd think I had just told him to go fuck himself. His face contorted back to anger and he yelled, "*You're lying! Let me in!!!*" He pounded at the door so hard, it felt like the glass was about to explode.

"I know he's in there!" he yelled.

"He's not!" I screamed back.

"If he's not there, then let me in so I can see for myself."

"No!"

From his vantage point, he could see pretty much our entire house. There was no way to visually separate myself from this man. I didn't know what to do, so I reached for the cord attached to the blinds and pulled them shut as quickly as I could—which, if you have ever dealt with vertical blinds, you know is still very slowly. First, they had to go across the length of the entire door, and then the other cord had to be pulled for the blinds to be fully closed. It was the slowest door slam in history, as he stood there ranting at me.

I heard him walk away. There was silence. He gave up. My body relaxed. I was safe. I had won . . .

Then came a *smash* from the other side of the house.

I knew exactly where he was.

On our front porch, there was a small window, covered by a screen that led into our laundry room. Whenever I was locked out, I'd push that screen in and crawl through the window. My guess was that he was trying to do the same thing. In this moment, the fear was different. I knew I couldn't hide. He was coming inside the house. I needed to do something; I needed to defend it and me.

As I ran to the laundry room, I grabbed a wooden ninja sword that I had "hidden" in an umbrella stand. First rule of being home alone: always have some "weapons" placed throughout the house in case of an emergency. Not that I had ever imagined a crazed friend of Hunter's being the attacker—I had always pictured a group of bikers, satanists, or satanist bikers (the most popular '80s movie villains).

This ninja sword was from last year's Halloween costume and actually wasn't a children's toy but a demo tool for martial artists who work with swords. It was made of solid wood like a skinny baseball bat. It could do serious damage without breaking. Never had I been so happy that my parents always went all out on Halloween costumes.

So with my sword in hand, I opened the laundry room door and saw half of this man in my house. The window was high off the ground, so to get through it headfirst, your feet would be off the ground on the other side. This was my moment, my chance to fight off this intruder while he was in a defenseless position, and I did. I started recklessly swinging at this man. He was totally defenseless, and I was just slashing at him with my sword and screaming, "He's not home!" The man blocked most of my blows with his hands, but I also got in some hard hits on his knuckles and some solid pokes in his chest, and then finally there was a loud *crack* as I clocked him straight across the skull.

Recognizing that, at this moment, he was the weakest he was going to be—dazed and stuck half in and half out of the window, like a home invasion version of Winnie-the-Pooh—I decided the safest option was to abandon ship. I dropped my sword, ran to the back door, unlocked it, and ran to the house of my next-door neighbor, Hunter's son. Hunter Jr. was the opposite of Hunter; he was sweet and funny, and he had a bodybuilder's physique. Arguably the nicest guy on the block. He had recently moved in and I knew he could help. I told him what was happening, and he called the police.

By the time the police arrived, the man had disappeared, leaving a note that simply said, "Hunter, call me," with a number scribbled below. My mom was stuck at work, so the police assured me they'd patrol the top of the street for the rest of the day. But as long as Hunter lived here, this guy would eventually come back—if not today, then someday, right? I was told not to worry about that, but it was impossible. I was still terrified.

Hunter Jr. walked me back to my house. He was already late for work, and he reminded me to lock the doors behind him—which I did. Then I went and checked all the windows, too. I returned to the laundry room. It was a complete mess, but it looked more like someone had had a bad laundry day rather than a home invasion. I picked up the window screen from the floor and popped it back in the window, then straightened up the laundry. I grabbed my fallen sword, now scarred with battle damage, and patrolled the house, rechecking all the windows and doors. Occasionally I'd exit the house, sword in hand, so I could see whether the police car was still at the top of the block, and it was.

When my parents came home, I gave them the note. I told them of the whole ordeal. "Wow, he sounds like a real crazy. Make sure you always lock the doors," they said. They picked up the shattered picture that had crashed to the floor earlier in the day, pulled out the remaining glass, and hung it back up on the wall—like nothing had happened. But something had happened!

I rebounded from these events quickly because I grew up in a family where if you survived, you were fine. If everything turned out okay, that was it: "Move on." The idea that there could still be lingering emotional trauma and fear didn't cross my parents' minds. It was just like the picture that was rehung on the wall: a casual observer might not notice anything, and you can pretend that nothing's wrong with it, but if you actually look at it, you see that it needs some attention. But this is how my mom and I had to survive.

Now that I'm a parent, I wrestle with the desire to fix things or minimize the trauma that my own kids feel. But I also know that acknowledging their fears and sitting with them in their anxieties are just as important. I give them a chance to express themselves without minimizing their emotions. I don't always get it right, and I'm trying to find that balance. After the school shooting in Uvalde, my oldest son came home from school and asked us, "Did you hear what happened in Texas today?" While this wasn't the first school shooting that he had been alive for, it was the first one he was aware of. We asked how he was feeling, and he told us he felt safe with all the protocols in place at his public school. It felt at first like he was trying to convince us that he was okay. So we just listened and let him tell us his experience of the events. We didn't race to make it okay or tell him how far he was from that school. We let him ask us questions, and we really wanted to center his experience and feelings, not ours—which was hard to do. As I tucked him into bed that night, we spent a longer time than usual lying there talking. All of a sudden, he said, "I'm scared." I fought everything in me that wanted just to make it better for him. I remembered how fearful and alone I felt as a child, and I knew it could be different. I said to him, "It's okay to be scared, but I'll always be here for you." I grabbed him, and he grabbed me tighter than ever. When he released, he smiled and said, "Thanks, Dad, I feel better." I think every kid wants to be Kevin McCallister, because they want to be home alone—but no kid wants to feel alone.

DYING AT DISNEY

I loved going on vacations with my dad because wherever we went there was always an amusement park. I honestly didn't realize till college that people traveled to places without roller coasters. *How is that a vacation? What do you do for fun?* These trips were escapes from my homelife; they were a chance to live carefreely, and we did everything with a reckless abandon. Our itinerary was always packed from morning to night with rides, water parks, buffets, haunted houses, fireworks, and always plenty of *ice cream*. Over the years we often found ourselves returning time and again to Disney World, which to me felt like a place where nothing could go wrong. Life was perfect there and I loved it.

So when I started feeling sick to my stomach just a few days before my dad and I were supposed to leave for our annual trip,

I was in denial. I couldn't get sick before a vacation. Didn't my body know this? Christmas, your birthday, federal holidays, these are not times when you can get sick! You needed to be in tip-top shape. But I wasn't, and I couldn't hide it—though I did try. I was afraid that my mom wouldn't let me go if she found out I was sick. Unfortunately, when I snuck into the bathroom to puke, it wasn't something I could do discreetly. She found me lying facedown on the floor. I tried to shrug it off, saying, "I just like lying down here because the floor is so cold!" She saw right through my lie, and my greatest fear was about to come true. As she put me to bed, I weakly asked, "Can I still go to Disney?"

Without missing a beat, she replied, "Let's talk about that later." Which is parent for no. I started to spiral; I couldn't miss this trip. I looked forward to these longer periods of time with my dad, and more importantly, the thought of being home with Hunter for an entire week seemed nightmarish. Plus I had big plans: I was going to ride Maelstrom, the newest ride at Epcot in the Norway Pavilion. It was based on the legends and lore of Norway's vast beauty and superstitions. How did I even know Epcot had a Norway ride? Because I read Steve Birnbaum's yearly guides to Walt Disney World like religious texts. I spent many a bus ride home from school with my head buried in a Birnbaum. While others read the master of horror, Stephen King, I read the master of Orlando, Stevie B. I studied maps of the parks like ancient texts. I read ride descriptions, memorized the best times to enter the parks, where to eat, and what not to miss. I had my guidebook marked up more than a Jared Leto script. These trips were important and I wasn't going to miss a thing. What kid doesn't want to get an up-close look at the deep-sea oil rigs that fuel Norway's bustling economy?

I did everything in my power to get better, which ranged from praying to lying. It was pure mind over matter, and after two days I was definitely on the mend. My mom grudgingly gave me the green light to go.

Disney World, here we come!

When we landed in Orlando, I was actually feeling pretty good. We decided to skip checking into our hotel and go straight to the park! We changed out of our winter clothes and into our Florida clothes in the Disney parking lot. We weren't going to waste a minute—Birnbaum would be proud. Once inside, I made a bee-line to get one of my favorite treats, the Mickey Mouse bar. It was a vanilla ice cream bar covered in chocolate that was in the shape of Mickey's head; now you can get one in any local supermarket, but back then, it was truly a one-of-a-kind treat only available at the parks. As a kid, this kind of ice cream construction blew my mind, and as a fan of Mr. Bill, the crude clay character from the 1970s *SNL* sketches, the bar was fun to eat because it was like I was eating Mickey Mouse alive. My dad made multiple videos of me eating the ice cream as he narrated the desperate pleas of Mickey: "No, please, I'm too young to die! Tell Pluto I love him."

We ran up to an ice cream seller, and I ordered one right away. As I took a bite, my normal world faded and my vacation in this magical place began.

"Oh no . . . !" my dad screamed in his best Mickey voice as I laughed through the bites.

This was quickly shaping up to be one of the best days ever—

and then, without warning, it wasn't. All of a sudden, I felt that familiar gurgle in my belly. *Oh no, not again.* It was always my stomach; this type of pain had started to become very familiar. "Can we sit down?" I asked. Please note: no kid has ever willingly sat down at Disney World. If you don't have a churro in one hand and a Fast-Pass in the other as you run to the Astro Orbiter, you are doing Disney World wrong. We hadn't even been on our first ride, and I already wanted to take a break. The cramps in my stomach were so bad that I couldn't stand up straight. I imagined my lack of balance was similar to the one I'd feel in the simulated 7.0 earthquake in the Disney–MGM Studio Backlot Tour's Catastrophe Canyon, which Birnbaum so vividly described.

I wobbled to the bench to catch my breath as my dad used this opportunity to try to conduct his best documentary-style interview on the VHS camera he had rented, but I couldn't play along. I was in too much distress. When I had these cramps, my mom's solution for this type of pain was "force a fart." I didn't know how to fart on command like a novelty act on the '80s show *That's Incredible!* But I tried. Nothing helped. I knew I was still sick but I couldn't admit it. So I mustered up the energy to go on a ride; maybe that would calm my stomach. Something nice and easy like the Pirates of the Caribbean. Unfortunately, I forgot that ride has a substantial drop. As we splashed down into the fictional Puerto Dorado for a leisurely boat ride through a waterside city under attack from marauding pirates, I felt like I was going to be spitting up as much water as Carlos, the kidnapped mayor who we watched being tortured in the local well as we sailed by.

I tugged on my dad's sleeve. "Maybe we should go to the hotel."

It took more fortitude than maybe anything else I'd ever done up to that point in my entire life to ask to leave the most magical place on earth of my own accord in the middle of the day. My dad looked at me, understanding the severity of the situation, and asked if I was okay. As Puerto Dorado burned in the background, I finally admitted, "I think I'm still sick."

As we drove back to the hotel, I was confused. I had been feeling better but then something changed and I didn't know why. But there was no time to think about that because my stomach kept getting worse.

We got to the hotel and I went right to sleep.

Hours had passed, and when I woke up, I was starting to feel like myself again. My stomach pain had receded, and now I was hungry. I had only had that ice cream bar all day. My dad didn't want me to be too active so we hit up room service. We ordered a feast: cheese ravioli, meatballs, pepperoni pizza, and of course, ice cream for dessert. I tore through it all. As we chowed down, I pulled out my Birnbaum and started to map out tomorrow's itinerary. I told my dad about a special new fireworks show, *IllumiNations*, which according to the book, told the story of Earth through explosions in the sky and was divided into three movements titled "Chaos," "Order," and "Meaning," emphasizing the idea of humanity as a single unified tribe on this planet. I marked that as a "must do." Little did I know the explosions were about to happen right in our hotel room.

Soon after I finished the meal, the stomach pains came back. I clutched my belly in pain. Something wasn't right. I'd never felt this way before. It was even worse than it'd been earlier. It felt like what the chest-bursting scenes in *Alien* looked like. But since I hadn't seen *Alien*, it felt more like the chest-bursting scene in *Spaceballs*. I was writhing back and forth on the bed, until I passed out.

I woke up like a shot, not knowing how long I'd been out. My dad was asleep on the bed next to mine. Then my body started to shake and, just like the finale of Indiana Jones Epic Stunt Spectacular, I *exploded*! Everything I'd eaten escaped my little eleven-year-old body. In seconds, I had created a Jackson Pollock–esque explosion in the hotel bed. My dad bolted up, and by the horrified look on his face, I could tell the situation wasn't good. As tears streamed down my face, my dad told me it was probably food poisoning. But I was confused: my dad had eaten the same stuff as me, and he wasn't sick. But I couldn't go there; that would mean there was a bigger problem. So I focused on the positive and tried to spin it to myself. *Okay, this is good, you aren't sick; it's just food poisoning. You'll be fine for the park tomorrow.* Even though I was covered in my own filth on both ends, I had only one goal: to get back to the park.

After a quick shower, I came out to see Dad, who'd done his best to clean up the mess. He took all the sheets, wrapped them up in a giant bundle of gross, and placed it in the closet. He put multiple trash cans around me and laid down extra towels so, if it happened again, I'd have a target. But I didn't think there was going to be a second round; I felt pretty good, and plus, what was left? I got into Dad's bed as he situated himself on the very comfortable chair. And I pulled out my dog-eared Birnbaum once again and started to read about Aerosmith partnering with Disney on a brand-new thrill ride called the Rock 'n' Roller Coaster. But as I read about the design of the super-stretch limo, I started to gag. An image popped into my head of that Monty Python sketch where the large man explodes because he ate too much, and I legitimately began to worry that maybe the same thing could happen to me. *Am I going to explode? Am I going to die?!?* But there was no time to meditate or obsess about death, because I needed one thing: *a bathroom*. But there was no time. I vomited *hard* all over my beloved Birnbaum book.

While I was coming to terms with the loss of my guidebook and the sneaking fear this trip wasn't going to be all I hoped for, there was a knock at the door. It was the hotel manager. "Is everything okay?" the manager asked from the other side of the door. "We received a noise complaint."

Dad scrambled. "Uh . . . We're fine! Sorry about the noise." But just as the manager walked away, Dad screamed, "Can we have more towels?" *Yeah, nothing suspicious about that.*

As my dad helped me to the bathroom, he told me, "We're going home." I was feeling so bad I couldn't disagree. The room was a mess. The Birnbaum was destroyed. Vacation was over. As we left the room, I surveyed all the damage: towels bunched and piled in the room like dirty snowdrifts in a mall parking lot. I felt incredibly guilty, seeing all this destruction. It was my fault. I'd wrecked the hotel room. Deliriously, I told my dad, "We need to tell them. I need to apologize." My dad, to his credit and to the credit of his credit card, had a different idea. We were just going to leave and not tell *anyone*!

I still wanted to help somehow, so I limply carried a bundle of gross linens into the hallway, the same way you might leave a room service tray for pickup. While disgusting, it served as a warning to all those who entered that inside was worse, and we snuck out of the hotel.

As we drove to the airport in the silence of the early morning, I remember Dad saying, "We'll never be allowed back into that hotel again." We burst out laughing, which I soon realized was incredibly painful due to all the unintentional ab work I'd been doing all night. But it was a glorious seven seconds. We had destroyed our room; we were hotel outlaws. I can't even imagine how they handled everything. If I owned that hotel, I would've just shut the entire hotel down. The whole thing. Forever unclean. But then again, it was Orlando; they probably dealt with this type of thing once a week. I bet that they had the room ready for someone by late check-in on the next day. God bless housekeeping staffs.

When we got to the airport, I was so weak that the skycap gave me a wheelchair. Since I wasn't going to make it to Disney, I was psyched to at least be in a ride-like vehicle. I found out years later that my dad thought my appendix had burst, and he didn't want me walking. Now if that was the case, I don't understand why he'd want me to go on a plane either, but we had bigger issues in front of us. He parked my wheelchair off to the side of the ticket counter while he settled the details of our trip. I sat there slumped over like Al Pacino at the end of *The Godfather Part III*. As if on cue, another skycap employee came up behind me and started pushing me deeper into the airport. I was so out of it that I didn't ask any questions. I assumed it was all part of the plan. It was not.

This skycap guy asked where I was going. I told him New York City, and he said we were going to be late. He started picking up the pace until we were racing through the airport. I asked for my dad, and the skycap told me, "Don't worry, I'm sure you'll see him when you're home in NYC." *Wait, what? But he's here!* Something was off but I was too out of it to put it together. So I just sat back and enjoyed the ride as the guy wheeled me farther into the airport, then out of the corner of my eye, I saw my dad racing after me. He stopped the man. Apparently, the skycap had taken the wrong kid. Maybe my dad was right to leave Orlando after all. If this was the airport, I can't imagine what the hospital was like.

The skycap excursion had taken what was left of my energy and left me drained. I was a rag doll, a shell of myself. We boarded the plane, and I snuggled into my dad, trying to sleep. I awoke to a flight attendant and a man standing over me.

That man was Nipsey Russell.

Who's Nipsey Russell? According to Wikipedia, he is an American comedian, poet, and dancer best known for his appearances as a panelist on game shows from the 1960s through the 1990s, including *Match Game, Password, Hollywood Squares, To Tell the Truth,* and *Pyramid.* His appearances were often distinguished by his recitation of short, humorous poems, which led to his being nicknamed the poet laureate of television. He had one of the leading roles in the film version of *The Wiz,* as the Tin Man.

Did I know any of this as a child? *Nope!* The flight attendant had brought him over to make me feel better. I could barely pick up my head, but Nipsey burst into a poem when I did:

Hey little boy. I hear you are feeling ill.
I hope you go to the doctor and get a pill.
I know you're sad, I know you're sick.
But don't you worry, son, this flight is quick.

This was, in many ways, a fever dream. I couldn't react to anything happening around me; I couldn't even give Nipsey a smile. I heard his poem and went right back to sleep. I'm sure Nipsey thought he was going to talk to a kid with the flu, but when he saw me, he must've assumed they wanted him to give me my last rites. To his credit, I've never forgotten that poem.

When we finally got back to NYC, I was rushed to my doctor, who needed to rule out appendicitis. He had me bend over the examination table, and then while I was in that position, he announced, "I'm just going to stick my finger inside here to see what's what." *Wait, what?* Hadn't I been through enough? But before I could ruminate on it any more, the doctor inserted his finger. Honestly, after a night when everything had come out, it was nice to put something back in. While it was novel for me to have a finger stuffed inside of me, the doctor was very casual and made small talk as he . . . read the braille of my rectum? I mean, I don't know what he was doing in there. He quickly announced, "Not appendicitis," which was good news—but his finger was still in my butt and it didn't seem like it was leaving. The doctor had an epiphany.

He pulled out and asked a simple question: "Do you get a lot of stomachaches?"

"Yes."

"When do they happen?"

I thought about it and said, "A lot of times after breakfast and after dessert."

"Do you drink milk with your cereal and eat ice cream for dessert?"

"*Uh-huh!*"

"You're lactose intolerant."

I didn't realize what that meant at first, but he explained: milk was bad. Ice cream, pizza, cheese—all off the table. Then it hit me, it was the Mickey ice cream bar that made me sick at Disney World. It was responsible for all of this. He explained there was a pill to help combat it, but the only way to really get better was to avoid milk and milk products at all costs. Not only did I get a diagnosis, but he simultaneously wrecked every future vacation plan. Disney World and all amusements parks were now a food minefield for me. I had no more real escapes—no places where I could be care-free. I'd have to be just as cautious on vacation as I was at home to protect myself and my body. Nothing was going to be the same.

I replaced my Birnbaum book with a bottle of Lactaid. When pizza appeared or ice cream was served, I stepped back. But there was a silver lining. Somehow I had said goodbye to the boy I was—obsessed with attractions—and instead, I became the attraction. In the eyes of my peers, I had aged decades on that trip. I was now a man—a man who couldn't eat dairy. I instantly became that mid-forties disgraced cop from movies I had always wanted to be. I had a history. And it wasn't pretty. Classmates would gather around me at birthday parties and pepper me with questions.

"So you can't have milk?"

"Nope?"

"What about ice cream?"

"Nah."

"Pizza?"

I'd shake my head no.

"Could you die if you don't have your pill?"

I'd lean back in my chair, pop a Lactaid pill in my mouth, take a hard swallow, and dramatically say, "Almost did."

WEIRD AL IS THE DEVIL'S MUSIC

"There is no Santa Claus, only Jesus!"

My aunt Barbara, Hunter's sister, delivered the news like a kill shot. She stared down at me, smiling vacantly as she sat on her piano bench preparing to play another hymn, and something in the way her heavily made-up eyes glared at me assured me she was telling the truth. The news stunned me, and I sat frozen in the living room as everyone went on with the Christmas Eve festivities. Was this true? Why wasn't anyone reacting? This was huge news, right? I was probably nine and had been holding out hope, longer than most, for the Big Man to be real. I never expected that the bubble would be burst not by a fellow classmate or even an older wisecracking cousin but by my born-again Christian aunt. Why would she do this? Isn't a core tenet of Christianity "Do unto others as you would have them do unto to you"? She wasn't just yucking my yum, she was outlawing it.

My mom and Hunter had been venturing deeper and deeper into born-again Christianity, and I was getting used to this type of behavior where people simply didn't practice what they preached. If you disagreed, spoke up, or asked questions that challenged their point of view, you'd be struck down. Everything felt punitive.

It was a culture shock for me as up till that point, I had grown up "textbook" Roman Catholic. We'd attend a mass on Sunday morning that got in and out in forty-five minutes, and then get jelly donuts on the way home. Although I never really looked forward to going to church, it wasn't that big of a deal. It was like tagging along to run errands with my parents, except that I couldn't wear shorts or sneakers.

Though both of my parents were religious, their religion didn't define them—at least, not at that point. But after my mom got married to Hunter, his side of the family took us down a born-again rabbit hole. It started slowly at first. Jim and Tammy Faye Bakker, the premier televangelists of the time, were constant fixtures on our televisions. A large leather-bound family Bible became a centerpiece on our living room table and others popped up throughout the house. We soon started going to a new congregation, about thirty minutes away from our house, and when I stepped inside, it was unlike anything I had ever experienced.

The Living Christ Church was wide and bright, and looked more like a gymnasium with carpeting than a church. Plus it was *packed*! Every Sunday we praised the Lord for a minimum of three hours. These masses never seemed to end.

The sermons fluctuated wildly between joyful and wrathful. Sometimes there were long periods of contemplative silence and other times the music played so loud that my ears would ring on the car ride home. The most unnerving thing, however, happened when the power of Christ became too much for the minister or any of the members of the congregation, and they would lose control over language and start speaking in tongues. I watched in shock as my family members looked like they were possessed, shouting a cacophony of gibberish into the air while their bodies writhed toward heaven. I saw preachers ball up their fists and release "*God* energy" to "heal" people; it was done with such force that the afflicted would collapse, fainting into other people's arms. Tears streamed down people's faces as they danced like your weird uncle at a wedding, just jumping up and down in the aisles. At the center of the pulpit was a large tank of water, and on certain weekends the minister dunked new believers, and the congregation furiously applauded in approval as the reborn came up gasping for air and spitting out water. And there I was, alone in this sea of frenzied people letting their freak flags fly, not understanding what was happening, like a classical music fan who stumbled into a Phish show.

Now, while my mom and Hunter were born again, my dad was still decidedly Roman Catholic. This meant when I spent the weekends at his house, I'd go to mass with him on Saturday evening (to beat the Sunday rush), and then he'd drop me back off at my house on Sundays so I could go to Living Christ Church with my mom and Hunter. Also during this time I went to Catholic school, where we'd have a midweek mass (or two), which meant I was putting in roughly seven to eight churchgoing hours a week. It was a lot. So I leaned in. I had no choice. Not only did I wear a cross with a crucified Jesus on it but also a scapular, which is like Catholic dog tags, the only difference being one tag hung in the front and the other in the back. It was always awkward when I took off my shirt at a pool party or in gym class and had to field a lot of questions about what these tags meant when, the truth was, I didn't even know. But I wouldn't take them off for fear that God might smite me if I did.

When my mom took away music deemed to be the work of the devil, including Weird Al Yankovic's *In 3-D* because it had a song called "Nature Trail to Hell," I didn't put up a fight. I was thankful that my mom had saved me from such a known devil worshipper. When fully posable Bible action figures replaced my He-Man toys, I quickly adapted and had Moses ride Battle Cat, and I used his Ten Commandments tablets as weapons. I even allowed myself to be "healed": Ever since birth my left foot has had an issue called "out-toeing" that causes it to splay out slightly when I walk. When I was a kid, doctors told me they would have to break my leg and reset it to fix me. I eschewed the doctor and went to the pastor of the congregation instead. I got in line at one of the services and waited my turn to be healed. When I reached the front, I had to tell this man what I wanted, not unlike a mall Santa. He heard my wish to fix my bum leg, and then he started praying, then the praying got faster. He reached his hand to the sky and then brought it down swiftly on my leg. Clamping it with his other hand, he started speaking in tongues as he shook my leg with such force that my entire body vibrated. When he released my leg he screamed, "YOU ARE HEALED!" I walked back to my seat and I didn't see any real change. My mom told me it would come. It didn't. I felt guilty. Why didn't the Lord heal my affliction? Was I not worthy? My biggest fear was coming true. I was embarrassed. I started to intentionally try to straighten it out when I was at services because I didn't want anyone to know the Lord had rejected me. I decided maybe I wasn't praying enough. So instead of just praying, I started performing my own masses out of my bedroom for no one, in the hope that doing a full service would get me forgiven more quickly. My leg never healed, and seeing that made me slowly start to question everything. Most importantly, why wasn't all this worship changing the chaos and abuse in our house? Hunter was the same guy he was no matter how many times the spirit of the Lord spoke through him. If anything, now I lived in fear of two people: one in the material world and the other on the spiritual plane.

I started to resent everything about religion, and I didn't want to go to church anymore. No one ever talked to me about it. They just assumed I wanted to sleep in on Sundays, not that I was being slowly driven to madness. I wanted out. Thankfully, after the fall of Jim Bakker and the collapse of PTL, we just drifted away from the Living Christ Church. No real reason was given, and honestly, I never asked. I was just thrilled to be out of that cacophonous circus, but the intense guilt and fear of godlike vengeance remained and were further drilled into me by years of Catholic school. There if the nuns hit you, you were told it was okay because they were servants of God. When I left home for college, I felt like I finally was free.

As an adult, I wrestled with what role I wanted religion to play in my life. At first, I rejected all of it. Then, as time went by, I went to different places of worship. During my visits, I'd list pros and cons in my head. Though I found pieces of each faith that resonated with me, unlike Goldilocks I couldn't find one that was just right. So I didn't commit to any of them.

When my first son, Gus, was born, my parents started asking

whether we planned to baptize him. For the first time in a long time, I had to answer to someone else about my faith. June and I managed to skirt around conversations about religion when it came time for our wedding, but this felt like a moment where we both needed to be united about the path we were going to set forth for our son. Thankfully, June and I were on the same page: we felt it would be disingenuous to get our child baptized when we weren't really connected to any church. My wife's father, a proudly religious man, suggested a compromise: Could he baptize Gus in our backyard instead? It was important for him to feel like our son was protected and looked after by God. We loved the idea, we thought it was a beautiful sentiment, and also we wanted to expand his protectors outside of the heavenly realm by inviting a small handful of people who were close to us. The day of the backyard baptism, I was overwhelmed by this profundity of love from all the people who joined us. By being there and experiencing this blessing, they were also agreeing to help be there and support us and our son as he grew. The ceremony was simple and personal and entirely our thing. I love that one of the ways we brought our child into the world was built around community, safety, and care—that's my religion. Those were things I wanted to embody and to instill in my children, and I never wanted them to feel unworthy of getting them—the way I felt when my foot wouldn't heal or when I prayed for help and no one came. I wanted my children to know that while we might not always agree, they were always cared for and loved, and whether or not they believed in Santa or listened to Weird Al wouldn't change that one bit.

HULK

As a kid, I loved watching *The Incredible Hulk*, the cheesy live-action '80s show in which the Hulk was played by two different people. David Banner—yes, they changed his name from Bruce to David—was played by Bill Bixby, a normal, nice guy. The Hulk was played by weightlifting champion Lou Ferrigno, covered in green paint and wearing a bad black wig. I loved the show except for the moments when David Banner would turn into the Hulk. The camera would zoom in on his eyes, and I watched in absolute terror as his pupils would shrink and then expand, changing into fiery cat's eyes. His anger was coming to a full boil, and you could see it all in those eyes. This transformation was one of the most horrific images my five-year-old brain had ever absorbed. I was watching someone literally explode from within. The first time I saw it, I ran out of the room crying. The image haunted me at night. My mom tried to get me over my fear by painting me green like the Hulk, but it wasn't the Hulk I was afraid of. I loved the Hulk. I was afraid of the split second when he turned—when man became monster.

I don't remember when the abuse started with Hunter. When I look back on that time, I just recall a chorus of raised voices, hurled insults, broken tchotchkes, and aggressive behavior. As I mentioned earlier, all the chaos and abuse were so normalized that only in the retelling do I realize just how abnormal they were. Those moments where I was so scared and thought I might die hit harder now because at the time I was just thrilled to survive. I felt victorious for outsmarting Hunter and narrowly avoiding a worse beating, like the time I outran a pitchfork he threw at my back. I didn't think about what would've happened if I'd run just a bit more slowly and he'd actually gotten me. Instead, those moments, though dark, feel triumphant to this day. They are the mental medals I won in the war I fought in my own house.

Most of the attacks happened without anyone else around, but sometimes other people were subjected to scenes of him punishing me. During a second-grade birthday party where I was "misbehaving," Hunter took a chair, placed it in the middle of the room, and spanked me in front of all of my friends. It wasn't with his hands; it was with a belt. As I lay across his legs, I saw sympathetic and confused looks on my friends' faces, and I tried so hard not to cry, to be relaxed as if this were an everyday occurrence. Truthfully, it was. The only difference was the presence of spectators. When he was done, I mustered all the energy I could to get back into the party, still shaking a bit but trying to convince everyone I was "fine," when I clearly wasn't.

As I got older, I realized more and more just how alone Mom and I were during that time. It wasn't that we wanted to stay; it was that we didn't have any help to get out. Over the years, we asked so many people to intervene. They were either scared to interfere or, as one relative put it, "we didn't want to intrude on your family business."

We tried to convince Hunter to go to family counseling for a long time, and when we finally succeeded, the therapist asked me to detail every violent physical interaction I'd had with him. Hunter wasn't allowed to interrupt; he just had to listen. As I told her every story of abuse I could remember, from washing my hands with scalding water until my fingers lost sensation to him routinely slapping my face and giving me wedgies that made my eyes tear, the therapist's shock was apparent. She eventually had to cut me off because the list was so long and she had more than enough to prove her point. She challenged Hunter: "Let's make an agreement: if you ever lay a hand on your stepson or wife again, I'm going to call the police." I believed her. Finally, we had someone who would hold him accountable.

He did hit me again. We all went back to the counselor. I told her exactly what had happened, and she took a long breath and said, "Okay, Hunter, this is your last chance. If it happens *one more time*, I'll call the police." She let him off the hook! She treated him like she had caught a kid stealing an Oreo from the pantry. I had never felt more helpless. I knew she was never going to call the police, and

I knew we were never going to family counseling again, because Hunter had gotten lucky, and he wasn't going to double down on his good luck. We left that office and never returned, and the therapist never followed up with us.

I once made an anonymous call to Child Protective Services that brought a police officer and counselor to our house. They interviewed Mom and Hunter together in the same room. It was like interviewing a kidnapper and kidnappee together: you aren't going to get the true story. My mom was too scared to say anything. Plus the counselor never spoke to me. Suffice it to say, CPS didn't find anything wrong—once again reinforcing the idea that if you live through it and have no scars, you're fine and why complain. I often thought, *Maybe one time he will break my arm or leg, then I can finally get some real help.* But he never did. That was the trickiest thing about his violence: it didn't leave any physically permanent marks.

But the most shocking thing was how neutral the rest of our family was toward all of the violence. My very Italian great-grandmother, who lived with us for a short time in her nineties, quickly became privy to what was happening at our house. I told her that Hunter hit me and my mom, and she said, "It's not abuse if nothing is broken." She'd lived through multiple wars and immigrated through Ellis Island—I often heard stories where she broke wooden spoons over her own children's heads when they misbehaved—so her empathy meter was probably a touch off. Once Hunter and I got into a physical fight where he threw a plant at my head, all while my great-grandmother sat there watching

TV, unmoved. Her only interjection was, *"Boys! Boys!* Keep it down! *People's Court* is on."

Unlike my great-grandmother, my grandma (my mom's mom) was my closest ally. I spent a lot of my youth with her while my parents worked. She was one of the only people I could fully confide in. She didn't like Hunter from the beginning; she'd joke and make fun of him to me privately and always made it a point to take him down a peg or two to his face in front of me. She was the only adult I ever saw do that. When she was over, we'd stand together. She always had my back—until she didn't. After a particularly bad Christmas dinner, a verbal fight started between my grandma and Hunter, and it slowly erupted until every adult was screaming. Finally, my grandma got up and announced to us, "It's either him or me!" If Hunter kept treating her grandson and daughter this way, she wouldn't come back ever again. The logic here is hard to parse: the punishment for his abuse was eliminating interactions with his mother-in-law . . . whom he didn't like? It made no sense and still doesn't, even though she stands by her decision to this day: "I had to do what I had to do"—which was nothing. She gathered up her coat and left, my grandfather trailing behind. We didn't see her again for what seemed like years.

My dad's response to Hunter was the toughest to come to terms with. Dad was *very* present in my life. The Herculean efforts he made to juggle work and fulfill his duties as a parent continue to astound me. He was my rock; though my parents were divorced and he lived and worked over an hour away, he never missed any of my big events. Not only did I spend every weekend with him, but he also came to our house after school twice a week just to be with me.

Hunter was jealous of my dad's relationship with me simply because my dad was my dad, and Hunter couldn't compete. In his warped brain, Dad was his greatest rival, and Hunter needed to take him down. He saw the joy I had in my eyes when Dad was around, a joy Hunter couldn't take away or duplicate. So in typical fashion if he couldn't earn it, he forced it—whether it was making me call him Dad, insisting on me giving him kisses, or talking shit about my dad and sharing things that my mom told him privately about her and my dad's relationship. It didn't work. I loved my dad and nothing was going to change that.

When I'd talk to my dad about Hunter and how he treated me, my dad would listen but never emotionally engage. I was so frustrated by his rational responses. I wanted him to be my defender. Unlike my grandma, he never expressed anger that this was happening to me, that I was subjected to this violence. He never made a move to change anything. I honestly don't think I've ever heard my dad talk badly about Hunter, even to this day. When it came to Hunter, my dad was always polite; their interactions resembled those of a worker and a building security guard who see each other every day, simple hellos and empty small talk. But this veneer of courtesy was eventually bound to break.

One Sunday afternoon, after a day of apple picking, my dad and I came home to see Hunter at the kitchen table in a bathrobe, drinking a cup of coffee. Dad and I entered like we'd done hundreds of times before and started chatting about our apple-picking adventure. Hunter sat motionless and then growled, "You come into my house and you don't fucking say hello to me?"

"It's your fucking problem if you didn't hear me say hello!" my dad responded almost instantaneously, as if he had been waiting for this moment for years. I'd never heard him curse before, let alone get confrontational.

Hunter was shocked that my dad spoke back to him and went into beast mode. He took his full coffee mug and threw it at Dad's head. Dad ducked as it exploded against the living room wall. Hunter then jumped up to his feet and charged at him. Given the violence I'd experienced at Hunter's hands, I was scared for my dad. I jumped in between them and was pushed to the ground as they grappled and clawed through the dining room and down our hallway. I scrambled to my feet, took some apples out of the bag, and fired them into the melee, hitting them both and making things worse.

The fight continued to our front door where Hunter slapped at my dad's face, knocking off his glasses, and pushed him out the door. As I lunged to follow, Hunter slammed the door shut, locking me inside while my dad was outside. In tears I sank to the floor and clutched Dad's broken glasses in my hand. Hunter pushed past me without a word, like a boxer after a match. I swung at his legs with my fists as he retreated to his bedroom and slammed the door behind him.

The fight was Hunter's ultimate attempt to take power away from Dad. Maybe Hunter thought that if I saw that he was the stronger one, I'd like him more. I was beside myself, but my mother had an idea to make it better for me and to keep the peace: a truce. She mediated an apology over the phone between these two men while

I listened in and got to tell them how much they upset me as well. But I'll never forget that as part of this truce my dad had to apologize for not properly greeting Hunter, and now as a result of that action, Dad would have to ask permission before he could enter the house every time he visited. In that moment my dad lived through a version of what my days with Hunter were like. Clearly, now things were going to change, be different. But no, things just went back to normal, like hanging that broken picture back on the wall. We never talked about it again.

Having no protection from the adults in my life started to awaken another person inside of me: someone who was stronger, who fought back, who had an antidote to Hunter's villainy.

I remember the day when I transformed. In addition to the acts of rage and anger, a lot of the abuse happened under the guise of playfulness. Hunter would lure me into a trap of just having fun, only to use my naivete to show me that he couldn't be beat. I often fell for the trap of "wrestling." He always wanted to wrestle, and I always took the opportunity because it felt like a chance to fight back without getting in trouble. But he was over forty years old, and I was ten. He dominated me. He wouldn't stop until I screamed or begged for mercy.

Then one day I was done begging. He had my arm twisted so badly it felt like it was about to snap, but I endured the pain. He kept repeating, "*Say mercy!*" and I wouldn't. I didn't want to be beaten anymore. As he sat on top of me, intensifying the pain, I saw a golden opportunity to overtake him. The way he was hovering over me, I had enough room to knee him in the crotch. It didn't feel fair, but I was over being fair. I kneed him twice in the groin, and he screamed in pain, a sound I'd never heard from him before. It felt good. He released his grip on me, and I rolled out from under him. I'd won! And I'd done it by being angry, fighting dirty. I could never beat him through strength alone; this was the only way. If I wanted a fighting chance, I had to be more aggressive, louder, dirtier. It was this moment that unleashed my inner Hulk—and gave me hope. My Hulk was my protector, the person I desperately needed but didn't have in my life.

But of course this change also had negative consequences. We began to fight harder. Soon every match was a no-holds-barred event. He'd choke me, covering my nose and mouth completely, and wait for me to almost pass out and then drop me on the floor and walk away. I got more and more aggressive, too; I used my fists and my words, whether it was making up songs on my Casio keyboard about his dead mother being a whore or starting a wrestling match where my only goal was to pull on his hair plugs. What I lacked in strength and size, I made up for in constant irritation, trying to hit him only where it hurt.

Another side effect was all this aggression started to bleed out into other areas of my life. If I was involved in a schoolyard fight, I'd take it *nuclear*. I fought like a person possessed. But no matter how much damage I did, the teachers assumed that I must have been provoked, because I wasn't "that kid."

I looked for fights, ways to work out this aggression. I saw myself as a vigilante chasing bullies. If I felt like someone was being disrespectful to me or a friend, my Hulk came out, and I challenged them like they were Hunter. Since they were seventh graders and I was used to fighting a forty-year-old man, I did more damage than was necessary. It's not something I'm proud to look back on now, because my fights were often incredibly violent. Then, as fast as the Hulk emerged, I'd go right back to being my calm self. The transitions between Bruce and Hulk were truly instantaneous.

Long after we left Hunter, my anger stayed with me. It reached its peak in high school when I sent a kid to the hospital. He had to get stitches after I wouldn't stop driving his face into a nearby car fender during our fight in the parking lot. I saw the look on the other kids' faces as they watched me pummel my classmate. It was the same look on my friends' faces at my birthday party when they saw Hunter whip me with a belt. I knew in that moment I'd gone too far. I saw the damage I was doing. I'd become Hunter. I was the aggressor. Years after Hunter was out of my life, this anger remained. Being bullied always brought it right back to the surface. I'd been lying to myself, saying that these kids deserved it. They didn't. I thought I had control over my rage. I didn't. Once it was unleashed, it took over, and my fuse was so short that I was actually dangerous.

I didn't want people to see me this way. I was embarrassed by who I was and what I did. I was out of control; I felt like a wild animal. I didn't have anyone to talk to, to help me work out what my anger and aggression were stemming from and how I might change. I knew deep down I had to walk away from reacting with violence, and I did.

My senior year of high school, a kid showed up to my house to fight me after I had been a total ass and prank called his mother about him being arrested. As we walked to the backyard to "fight," I had an out-of-body experience. I wasn't turning into the Hulk; I was the Hulk. I didn't want people showing up at my house just to fight me. I didn't want to be like Hunter who would come home in an arm splint or with a black eye because he said the wrong thing to someone in the truck depot. In that moment, I knew I needed to change.

Before a fight, I was used to feeling like a wild animal, but now my posture became that of prey. My voice cracked as I said, "I don't want to fight you." I felt tears welling up, as I finally admitted to myself that this wasn't me. I was a mess; in this moment I was reconciling with all my past aggressive behavior and was proud and scared about making a choice to break this pattern.

Then I did something I very rarely did: I apologized. "Hey, man, I'm really sorry. I fucked up. I didn't mean to freak out your mom." It was hard; in my household, there wasn't much apologizing going on. Apologizing meant you were wrong. If someone else was responsible for your behavior, then you never had to be accountable for anything. Occasionally, you might apologize for how heated you got but never for getting upset in the first place. But in this moment, the other kid's defensive posture dropped, and we were just two kids standing in my backyard. He gave some sort of warning, like "I'll let you off this time," as he walked away. But I couldn't even hear him because my heart was racing so fast that the sound of my pulse clogged my ears and I was in a bit of a daze. *Was this actually happening? Did I walk away from a fight? Was I finally leaving this part of me behind?*

After that day, I did a 180 and went in a completely different direction. I made it a point to avoid all fights and arguments. If someone else got angry, I took the blame. I was passive and rational. I was mirroring that part of my dad that frustrated me so much, but in doing so I wasn't getting better—I was just putting off actually dealing with any emotions. I still had this explosive berserker energy under the surface, but I knew how to keep it locked up. Occasionally, it would manifest suddenly, like on the subway with a pushy passenger or with a landlord I once attacked with a small potted plant (thankfully, I missed).

Before my long-term postcollege girlfriend broke up with me, she wanted us to go to couples therapy, which I happily did because I would agree to anything and, honestly, that was part of our problem. The relationship ended, but I stayed in therapy, finally working through the rage issues that I'd spent years avoiding. I realized I went from full-time Hulk to just Bruce Banner. There was no balance, just extremes. As I started to allow myself to examine these feelings, I found a new voice, less passive, more opinionated, someone who was okay with anger as a part of the spectrum of emotions I could access.

Years later when I was with June and we were talking about children, I felt scared. I'd always wanted to have kids, but I also knew that being a parent would be the truest test of who I was. I was afraid that the stress of parenting would upset the delicate balance I had found and that I'd worked so hard to achieve.

What if my anger came back? I had met June post-therapy, and she might have seen tiny moments of this in our time together, but she didn't really know that side of me. So bringing her into this fear was the final step of owning who I was, for better or worse. But she wasn't scared. She was there for me. When I think I'm in my darkest moment, knowing I have a partner I can express this to makes everything less scary, and she can relate to my darkness. With the knowledge that I was more aware and emotionally evolved than Hunter and with the right support behind me, we decided to have a baby.

When I met our son, I was instantly overcome with love for this precious being. My desire to protect kicked in again; only this time, I knew that part of protecting June and my son was not doing anything stupid that would scar them or put myself or them in danger. I still experience anger and even moments of rage, but I'm not afraid of that side of myself anymore. My anger might get the better of me sometimes, but it will never get the best of me.

THE GREAT ESCAPE

It was just a normal Wednesday, the house was quiet because Hunter was on vacation, and little did I know my entire life was about to change.

"PAAAAUULLLL!"

The sound of my mother's voice echoing through my childhood home always prompted a Pavlovian response in me. Instantly, my body tensed, my face grimaced, and my head rocketed backward as I released a primal "*uuugggggh!*" to the heavens from deep inside my body and then screamed back, "WHAAAAT?!"

"*Come here!*" she yelled.

"*Why?!?*" I volleyed back. I waited a beat; no response. We'd reached a stalemate. Now the choice was clear: get up and walk down the hall to deal with her face-to-face, or ignore her and deal with the wrath of a mother left unanswered. I yelled, "Coming!" as I approached her room.

My mom was in her fully carpeted master bathroom—yes, she had a carpeted master bathroom, which I always thought was classy as a kid and now realize is straight-up disgusting. "I want to talk to you," she said as she waved me over to take a seat on the tub's edge. I watched her as she applied mascara to her lashes and, without turning her head, caught my eye in the mirror. "I'm getting a divorce," she said. "Would you like that?"

I was shocked. "Do you mean it?" We'd escaped for short times over the years, to hotels, to relatives' houses. "We aren't going back," my mom and I would whisper to each other in the darkness of night in whatever place we wound up in. "This is it. It's over." But every escape ended the same way. Hunter would find us, he'd make up with Mom, and we'd pack up and go home. Things would be better for a few days, and then, before you knew it, things were back to normal. Nothing ever changed for very long. We eventually stopped even trying to escape; in many ways, we'd both reconciled ourselves to this life or so I thought.

Something about this was different. In the past, these decisions to escape were made in the heat of the moment, in the middle of a fight, truly in fear for our lives. But this wasn't reactionary. It seemed measured, calculated. As a matter of fact, her relationship with Hunter had been in an upswing. What I didn't know at the time was that Mom was not only working up her courage to leave: she was also secretly working two jobs on the side, scraping together money to create a buffer so we could escape and not come back. She had lulled him into a false sense of security, and she was waiting to strike.

I had only one question: "When?"

* * *

Decades have passed since I've seen Hunter; he seemingly has been erased from my entire family's lives; no one mentions him; I'm even hard-pressed to find photos of that time. My mom and I will occasionally talk about what we went through together, and while she's always open to discuss it, we don't do it often; it's still sensitive and that's okay. I know where she stands. But on my dad's side, much went unaddressed for years. I never pushed. It wasn't until I was in my twenties, when I was going to therapy, that I realized we never spoke about what happened all those years with Hunter. When I finally brought it up, our first conversation probably caught him off guard. I had done all this work and reflection for months, and there we were at City Crab, a midlevel seafood restaurant in New York, when I dropped the bomb—"Let's talk about Hunter"—over a plate of fried calamari. A look of genuine shock came over his face as I told him what Mom and I had gone through, the look of horror and pity and disbelief you'd get from someone who hadn't been there. But he had been. He just kept saying, "I didn't know." But he must have known something; he had heard my stories, and he had even been in a fistfight with the man. It was odd, but I left that talk at City Crab feeling fulfilled simply because Dad and I had spoken about it; that step alone was so big that, in the moment, it felt like enough.

Becoming a dad changed my perspective on the events of my

childhood. I stopped thinking about myself living through abuse, and I imagined my sons going through that same thing at the hand of a stepfather. I asked myself how I would react to my kids telling me the stories that I told my dad. What would I do? The answer was always: I wouldn't just do something, I'd do everything. As much as I love my dad, I was finding myself angry at him for the first time. So I reached out again. Sadly, I've found that in the decades that have passed since our first conversation, his memories have gotten fuzzier, and now he continues to blame everyone but himself: "I didn't think it was that bad," or "I thought you were exaggerating," or even, "I thought your mom would be able to handle it, 'cause she told me she could." Now years later I'm finding the small amount of progress we made in our first conversation has taken a giant step back.

It was hard to get anywhere in these conversations. I've needed to ask myself, "What do I want from this?" What I really wanted from my dad was emotion, some connection to his part in this. I wanted him to be pissed; I wanted him to feel badly; I wanted him to be sorry without me telling him to be sorry. I wanted him to take responsibility. But how could I expect that from someone whose way of dealing with it seems to be not dealing with it? So I left our last conversation by simply saying, "When you are ready to talk about this more, I'll be here."

That was many years ago. We never discussed Hunter again.

It's understandably hard to talk about this stuff. There is no quick fix or simple apology. You can't just move on from it or be done talking about it. It's a part of my life. I imagine acknowledging my pain makes my dad and others who were around me during that time have to reckon with their parts in it, too. In my case and, as I imagine, in many cases of abuse, I was failed by people who loved me. They didn't know how to be, or didn't want to be, responsible. Not speaking about it created a subconscious shame and embarrassment deep within me about what I went through. *Why wasn't I worthy of being saved?* For a long time I kept it in; I didn't want to make this part of my story. It was too dark; it made people feel badly. But not acknowledging my trauma took away my triumph. I survived. I want to make surviving the abuse part of my story. I want to wear my former shame with pride.

Sometimes I'll share these stories with someone and they'll say, "How could you forgive your parents?" I'm not looking for someone to blame. That's black-and-white. I've found peace in knowing that I can't and shouldn't penalize anyone for who they could have been, least of all my mom and dad. Judging them for what they couldn't do then, and even what they can't do now, doesn't make anything better. Their inaction does not define them because they also did so many great things and I love them both, and I cherish the relationships I have with them. And selfishly, as a parent, I would want some of that slack, too. In case my kids write a tell-all book about me in 2059, I want to instill in them that I'm always going to be there for them, and I'm going to mess up, and when I do, I will be empathetic, I will apologize, and I'll do better. Most importantly, I'll keep talking with them until they feel better. So far, it's working.

* * *

It was the day of the escape, and my mom had planned it perfectly. She had gotten Hunter out of the house for a few days by convincing him that he had won a contest and the prize was a hunting trip in Montana. This gave us enough time to pack and get out before he got back, or so I thought.

As the last few boxes were being loaded up in the moving van, Hunter pulled into the driveway. My mom pulled off an *Ocean's Eleven*–style heist, right under his nose, complete with a final face-off between the heroes and the villain. Finally, we got the upper hand over a man who'd always had the upper hand over us. This was our moment to take the power back. How was he going to respond?

My mom told him she was leaving, and I watched hungrily for his reaction. It was unlike anything I could have predicted: he didn't beg or cry or even seem to care that we were leaving. Instead, he harassed the movers: "Why are you taking that?! Leave that here!" He started unpacking boxes that sat in the driveway, looking for his stuff. Maybe he saw the writing on the wall, and if he couldn't save his marriage, he could at least save the dinning room table. We let him keep a large portion of the limited amount of stuff we'd planned to take. It was a small price to pay.

It was finally time to leave, and we got into Mom's tiny Volkswagen Rabbit, which was packed to the gills with everything that we didn't have time to box up. We were an ignition turn away from freedom, when Hunter put himself in front of the car.

"Don't go," he said. His voice was low and quiet. His calmness scared me more than his anger ever had. We pulled around him. "*Gail!*" he screamed, his voice echoing through the dead-end street. He started chasing the car. As he caught up, he banged on the driver-side window.

Mom hit the brake. *No!* I thought. *Not again! We can't stop now.* But we did.

Mom rolled down the window. He looked at us and said, "I want my guns back!" In my lap were two guns, a shotgun and a BB gun; both were mine. I had put them in the car for protection, an upgrade from my wooden ninja sword. He reached through the driver's window and grabbed them by the barrels, and trying to stop him, I grabbed the stocks. We created a firearm tug-of-war across my mother as she screamed at us both to "Let go." I didn't want him to take the only thing we had to protect ourselves. But then looking at my mom over the barrel of the gun, something clicked. *Let go.* It's the one thing we couldn't do this entire time, and now I was inadvertently anchoring us here. So I did it. I let go of the guns, and in that moment we were released from this cycle of violence that we had grown so accustomed to. He could have his weapons but he couldn't have us.

Hunter stumbled backward with my guns in hand. My mom hit the gas, and we pulled away. I didn't turn around to see the look on his face. As we drove off the block where I'd spent most of my childhood, I didn't know exactly where we were going, but I knew for the first time, I'd be okay.

Part 2

THE NEW TESTAMENT

SHoW WORLD

My first realization that I might be behind the eight ball regarding sex was when I referred to it as "making love." A girl in my seventh-grade class looked at me disdainfully and announced, "You mean fucking!" Everyone laughed, but I had never heard that term, and it seemed so angry. What was fucking?!

Sex wasn't often discussed in my house; I never got "The Talk." I just got little factoids intermittently from my mom, like when she showed me a picture of herpes on a penis in a medical journal and announced, "That's what happens when you have oral." I didn't even understand what oral was, but I wasn't going to be having it.

What I knew about sex was often learned directly from the playground. A friend showed me the word *smegma* in the dictionary.

He looked at me wide-eyed and said, "All girls have this!" Another classmate told me a condom, which he called a rubber, was when you took the eraser part of a pencil off and shoved it in your pee hole before having sex to prevent the girl from getting pregnant. Seemed plausible enough, albeit *extremely* painful. When I finally learned about oral, a distant cousin told me that a blow job was a complex sex act that required a handful of ice and a hair dryer. Then he described a homemade version of Icy Hot on a penis. When my mom overheard me telling this to my friend, she called me a "pervert" and grounded me without also letting me know that what I was saying was totally false.

My dad didn't offer any take. I remember loving a movie called *Club Paradise*, with Robin Williams and Peter O'Toole. It's essentially a movie about a mom-and-pop Club Med. During the film, one character says, "Your visitors are fucking so much in the pool you're going to have to be cleaning diaphragms out of the pool filters." Now I knew about fucking but had never heard about diaphragms. I asked my dad, "What is a diaphragm?" He explained that it was how we breathed, and it was a muscle that helped our lungs. A horrified look crossed my face, "So, do they come out when you have sex?!" At first, he was confused, and then I recounted the scene for him, to which he replied, "You are too young to worry about that!" Which further convinced me that a piece of my body came out during sex. I was mortified. I was like a detective chasing a serial killer named Intercourse. I didn't know much about him, but I was learning his habits and putting together clues daily, and 80 percent of them were wrong.

My last hope for an honest discussion about sex should have come from my high school sex ed class. The only problem was that I went to a Catholic school, and we didn't have that option. We had "Health," which was taught by our gym teacher. Sex ed was a small part of that class. Instead, he focused on other things like how to wash our "pits, franks, and beans" (his terms), which in retrospect seems to be pretty self-explanatory and not something that required multiple lectures. Once a boy asked about periods, and the gym teacher quickly shot back, "That's a girl's private business and none of yours." Then he high-fived a girl like he was protecting her honor. The closest we got to sex talk was a call-and-response he taught us, where he would say, "The only safe sex is," and then point at us, and we'd shout, "No sex!"

Sex seemed like a minefield of responsibility, contraptions, and diseases. As much as I wanted to have it, it totally stressed me out. So I was happy to avoid it. But I needed to learn more about it, and I wanted to see it. In the summer between my sophomore and junior years, I spent much of my time hanging out at friends' houses. Most of my friends' parents worked, and we were at an age where we were allowed to be at another kid's house without their parents being home, which allowed us to do whatever we wanted as long as we got back before they returned from work. One day, we got the idea to go into New York City and watch an X-rated movie—finally we were going to get some answers. It was like a sexual field trip, an adult day out. Brian, John, and I walked to the Long Island Rail Road and headed into the Big Apple.

Exiting the subway, we came face-to-face with . . . the Disney

Store. It was huge, and we momentarily delayed our day of debauchery for a side quest. We entered and I marveled at the store—the lights, the displays, and all the unique toys. I ran over to a Jiminy Cricket plushie; I had never seen one at any of the Disney parks, and I wanted it badly. I decided not to buy it because clutching a stuffed animal while watching an X-rated movie didn't scream *adult*. We left the Disney Store empty-handed and committed to a more mature day in the city.

Back in the streets of Manhattan, the first thing we noticed was the lack of adult movie theaters. We decided to get a beer to regroup.

We walked into a bodega and examined the beer case for far too long. What should we be drinking? The answer was clear: Colt 45! We opted for malt liquor not because it was cheap and strong but because we were all Star Wars fans. We loved that this was the beer Lando drank, or at least that's how it appeared since he was in all those Colt 45 commercials we grew up with. As we approached the counter with our 40s, the cashier said, "ID."

Damn!

We should have thought through this part of the plan. We knew that you needed to be twenty-one to drink. We assumed that in the city it was different. It was not. We came up with an excuse that we'd left our IDs at home, and I added, "We go to NYU." Without hesitation, the cashier scooped up the three large bottles and sent us on our way.

We needed IDs? We thought the city was lawless and we could get anything we wanted whenever we wanted. But the truth was that without IDs, we were done. We had been in the city for less than thirty minutes, and our plans had completely fallen apart. We dejectedly started walking down Forty-Second Street when John said, "Look." He pointed at a tattered sign hanging from a yellow aluminum awning, which said "We Make IDs." It was a sign from God, a sex god. We entered the small store, which sold a mix of tourist souvenirs, camera goods, and luggage and had a small area in the back for IDs. We approached the skinny person at the counter watching a small black-and-white TV. He had a pencil behind his ear and didn't even look up as we approached. I whispered, "We are here for IDs"—as if this service wasn't advertised on the front of the store and this man wasn't sitting under a sign that said "We Make IDs."

He sized us up and said, "Twenty . . . each." As we handed over our money, I tried to make some small talk to further convince the attendant that these IDs were on the up and up. "We left our regular IDs in our dorm, and we don't want to go back because . . ."

He cut me off: "What school?"

It was all happening so fast. "Um, NYU?"

He pulled the pencil behind his ear and scribbled *NYU* on a notepad.

"Age?"

I blurted out, "Twenty-one?"

He wrote down *twenty-one*. Then Brian pulled me over into a tête-à-tête with him and John: "That's too obvious."

John agreed. "Tell him twenty-two."

I reapproached the counter man. "Actually, twenty-two. My birthday is this week, and I figure, let's keep it up-to-date."

I stepped on a ratty red *X* made of masking tape on the floor. He pulled a giant Polaroid camera from under the counter and snapped a picture. Then he announced, "Next." He did the same for Brian and John and then sat in front of a typewriter. He inserted each card into the typewriter, entered our information, and then our pictures were cut out and placed in the IDs. He fed them through a laminating machine and, within minutes, we had become three twenty-two-year-old NYU students. (Don't judge, we had had a gap year.)

We stepped out onto the street, each twenty dollars lighter but with our spirits lifted. We examined our new IDs. They literally said "COLLEGE IDENTIFICATION." There was a blank space that said "I am a student at," and beneath that "New York University" was typed in, as if NYU had decided to outsource production of its IDs to a blanket college ID place. Apart from the fact that the photos showed us in the same clothes we were currently wearing, they seemed perfect.

We admired our IDs in front of the store, wondering what we should do as freshly minted twenty-two-year-olds. Go back for those Colt 45s? But before we could decide, a young guy approached. He probably was an actual twenty-two-year-old, so to us he looked like a thirty-five-year-old. He whispered, "You all looking for a good time?" Since I already clearly enjoyed being conspiratorial, I whispered back, "Yeah."

He asked what we were up to and I confidently but secretly announced, "We're going to see a porno; know any good spots?" I'm sure my use of the term *porno* labeled me as someone who had never seen one. His eyes lit up. "You wanna see beautiful ladies?"

We jumped at this: "*Yes!*" (This was better than we had planned.)

"I can show you."

"Really? Do we need IDs?!"

He looked at us quizzically. "No."

"Oh cool, just checking. 'Cause we totally have them."

Before we could wallow in not being carded, our new friend took off and waved for us to follow. He moved quickly, and we struggled to keep up as he pointed out his version of New York City landmarks. "That place sucks . . . I hate that guy . . . See that place? Don't go there . . . That dude is a thief." It was a private tour of one man's petty grievances in his neighborhood, and we nodded and took it all in as if we were on an architectural tour of the city.

We kept walking farther and farther, and the neighborhood started feeling a lot more sketchy than the bustling Forty-Second Street. As he walked us farther away from people, he kept peppering us with questions. "You're not from here, are you? How much money do you guys have?" Then he pointed down an alley. "It's just down here in that back building."

Something wasn't right.

I stepped outside myself and could see what was happening, and it wasn't good. We were three young kids alone in the big city. No matter what our IDs said, the acne on our faces told a different story. For the first time, I looked at our tour guide, noticing that his sweatshirt was dirty, as if it hadn't been washed in a long time, or ever, and that his shoes were untied and different from each other. Common sense finally kicked in: *This is not safe.* I'd seen many a "very special episode" of my favorite sitcoms growing up warning me of scenarios just like this.

I stopped in my tracks and called out, "Wait!" Everyone stopped. I knew we were in danger but now we needed a plan to escape. My friends were confused and looked at me like, *What the hell?* as our tour guide came closer and questioned, "What's up? I thought you guys wanted to have sex?"

Wait! Was that what we were doing? I just wanted to see naked people. I wasn't ready for sex. I paused. I fumbled my words but managed to say, "We're good. We gotta get back home . . . I mean to our dorms." My friends looked at me like I was crazy. I tried to implore them with my eyes and a headshake. "Right, guys?" There was an awkward standoff. I yelled, "*Run!*" and took off, and my friends followed behind. When in doubt, I went back to a classic Paul Scheer move. Run now and figure out the rest later. The man gave chase as we dodged people and piles of trash to get back to a more populated area. He gained on us. Was he going to mug us or force us to have sex? Each scenario was equally scary. He gave up as we got closer to Times Square and were engulfed in a crowd of people. Finally, we were safe. Our chests heaved as we leaned against the side of a building, catching our breath. It was obvious we all had been feeling the same way, but no one wanted to be the person to cut our sexual field trip short. We all had had enough for one day. The desire to go home was strong.

Then a man dressed as a circus ringmaster approached us and said two magical words: "Naked ladies?" He passed a flyer into each of our hands. "Come on in, gentlemen!" The man gestured to a large building with a marquee behind him. Bright lights flashed, and a giant sign announced, "Adult Movies 25¢, Live Girls, X-Rated."

Reflective glass and posters of beautiful women seemingly lined the inside of the space.

Although we had just gotten duped, we had come all this way to see naked women. Yes, this man was dressed in a circus costume, *but* he appeared way more trustworthy than the man we had just escaped from, plus this one's place of business wasn't down a dirty back alley. "What do you say, gentlemen? Wanna see a show?"

He asked for our IDs. He examined each one for about a milli-second and gave us a big smile that said, *I know this is fake, but I don't care.*

"Looks good to me," he said. He opened the door. "Welcome to Show World, gentlemen." We walked up the stairs—our adult day had finally begun.

I had never been in a strip club, an adult theater, or anything else like this. Walking up the staircase into Show World, we sud-denly felt like we were being transported into a new realm. With every step we took up the stairs, less natural light got in, and now we were in this place of multicolored bulbs, odd sounds, and circus colors.

The main floor we arrived on was like a Grand Central Station of adult activities. Show World wasn't a traditional adult theater. It had more of a carnival vibe. There were doors and signs to different rooms. We wanted to fit in with the clientele, but we relaxed when we realized that the other people didn't care who else was there as long as we didn't look at them. The less eye contact, the better.

In front of us were a bunch of doors around an octagon. One door was open, and a janitor was inside, mopping the floor. He exited and said, "All yours." Since we didn't have a plan, this invitation was the best opportunity to begin our adventure. We entered and closed the door, and it was dark except for a green light. From countless hours at Chuck E. Cheese, we knew money went into that slot, and a lot of it. It was ten bucks, which was a lot of money, but it was too late to be frugal. We put our money into the slot, and a steel curtain rose, revealing a naked woman on the other side. We thought we were about to see a movie, but this was a real-life human behind the window. What was this? It was like being in a bank, if the teller behind the glass was naked.

Then we realized we weren't the only people looking through a window. There were a bunch of almost-blacked-out windows going around the octagon. We watched as the woman made her way over to our window and stared at us; she whispered, "Hi!" We stood frozen in a way that begged the question of who was looking at whom. Before we could understand what we were watching or supposed to do, the steel curtain that had come up so quickly came down even faster. *We just saw a naked adult!* We celebrated.

Now what? As far as I was concerned, we had accomplished our mission. Plus ten dollars was a lot of cash for something that felt way shorter than playing a game of *Dragon's Lair*, which had an equally expensive cost-to-gameplay ratio. We needed to spend our remaining money wisely. I still had a twenty. My friend remembered the sign that mentioned twenty-five cents. That was more our price point. He went to find that, and my other friend followed. We split up, saying, "Let's meet back in fifteen minutes." It was an arbitrary time, but it felt right.

I was overwhelmed by choices. I felt a hand on my shoulder. I tensed up, assuming it was a security guard that was about to kick me out, but when I turned, I found myself staring at a beautiful woman in a robe. Then she got very close to my face. "Come with me . . ." She grabbed my hand as we walked together down a hallway. She brought me into a room and told me to sit. I did.

She then looked me in the eyes and said, "Want to watch me take a shower?"

What?! My eyes felt like they were going to pop out of my head. Was this a thing? Was a shower a standard option? To my chaste brain this seemed so wildly out of the norm. It felt downright perverted. In my mind, taking a shower was personal and the least sexy thing you could watch anyone do. I quickly said no, in a way that was saying, *I assure you, madam, I'm not a pervert. I just came here to see traditionally naked women doing normal sexy things and not acts of hygiene.* I got up and told the woman I had to meet my friends, and I took off out of the room. I needed to escape this world. I wasn't ready. I had flown too close to the sun. I knew too much and nothing at all.

I saw both of my friends in video booths. I tapped on their shoulders and announced, "I ran out of money. I'll be outside." They waved me away, which I guess anyone might do while watching pornography. I ran down the multicolored staircase until the natural light started to seep in, and I was back in the real world.

The doorman saw me and said, "So soon?" I tried to play it cool. "Oh yeah, just a quickie," I said, not even registering the image I created with that double entendre. I sat on a fire hydrant and waited. Time seemed to go slowly, but I'm sure no more than ten minutes passed, and my friends finally exited.

"That was awesome!" they crowed. I agreed. They told me about the movies they had watched, and I lied and told them, "Oh, yeah, well, I watched a woman take a shower!"

"*What?!*" they roared with excitement. "You could do that?"

"Yes, and I did. No big deal." I shrugged.

"We gotta come back!" they said. I agreed, but truthfully, I never wanted to go back there again.

We walked back to the subway station. I still had twenty dollars burning a hole in my pocket, and before we went through the turn-stile, I said, "Wait here." I ran back to the Disney Store, marched to the giant plushie centerpiece, and grabbed that Jiminy Cricket. I needed him after all.

MIDDLE SCHOOL MOGUL

"I *think* I can get you an interview."

"Really?"

"Stay by your phone."

This was the call I had been waiting for, the moment that could change my life. Blockbuster Video, the premier video rental store, had a job opening, and my friend Ajay had an in. Not only was this the most coveted after-school job, but it was also my fantasy; working at a video store was like winning the lottery. This was in the early nineties. It was the beginning of the era of Kevin Smith and Quentin Tarantino. All great new Hollywood careers started at a video store. So, you are goddamn right that I would stay by my phone, 'cause there were no cell phones, and that's what we did. I stayed by my phone and waited.

Trips to the video store were my lifeblood, and not just because I used them to rescue me from would-be attackers who wanted to steal my bike. I just loved being surrounded by all these movies: so much to watch, so little time. The best part was that no matter who you were or what you did, if you wanted some home entertainment, you had to go to the video store and take your chances just like everyone else. Maybe you went in looking for Al Pacino in *Carlito's Way*, but you were forced to leave with Pauly Shore's *Son in Law* (which, to be fair, is surprisingly funny). What you wanted didn't matter; all that mattered was what was left. So, on a Friday, when video stores were the busiest, you did everything possible to get there early enough to get your first choice. I would game the system to ensure I always got my first-choice rental. I would go to the video store on a Thursday and hide a copy of the movie I wanted on Friday, say Wesley Snipes's *Passenger 57*, behind a copy of a film no one wanted, like *Newsies* (sorry, Christian Bale). The thought was that no one would be renting *Newsies*, so the VHS tape would sit there untouched until I returned on Friday, at which point I'd grab the hottest new release and confidently bring it to the counter like a prospector who found gold—much to the shock of the other customers and even the clerk. I lived for these moments, beating the crowds and getting my perfect weekend movie. You might be wondering why I didn't rent it on Thursday. Because it was a twenty-four-hour rental, you idiot. I had homework and school on Friday. There was no time to watch the video until the weekend. When I was in high school, video stores were thriving—they were my favorite spot to hang out—but it hadn't always been that way.

My dad was an early adopter of VHS, and when he first got his machine, video stores were rare. Every Friday night, my dad would pick me up from my mom and Hunter's house for the weekend, and on the way to his apartment, we'd always stop at the one video store in the area. We were a part of a select club and it felt cool. The first store I remember going to wasn't even set up like a regular rental place. They kept the movies behind a glass window; you could only stare at them and never touch them, like expensive jewelry. If you saw something you liked, you'd have to look at the letter and number taped to the VHS box and then approach the counter and ask, "Do you have N34?" Then the clerk would go behind the counter and see whether it was there. If you were lucky, you were getting *The NeverEnding Story*; if you weren't, it was back to the glass cases, and the process would start all over again. The first stores had only one copy of each movie, so the chances that you'd see a new release before it was an old release were small. You'd have to put your name on a list and wait for a call from the store, like waiting for a kidney, and if you couldn't pick it up when they called, you went to the bottom of the list. It was cutthroat.

Loyalty was key. We were in a lot, so my dad and I became friends with the local video store guy. He'd occasionally hold a film for us, and this was my first taste of a video clerks' power. They were kingmakers. The friendlier we got, the more perks we received. He knew I loved Eddie Murphy. One day, as he packaged up our movies, he slid over a twelve-inch cardboard cutout for *Beverly Hills Cop 2* and said, "It's yours!"

I remember asking in disbelief, "Really?"

He replied, "Yeah, I was going to toss it in the garbage anyway."

One man's trash is another boy's obsession. I treasured this little piece of cardboard. It connected me to the world of movies, because you'd usually see standees only in movie theaters. And now I had one, too, even though it was 1/100 of the size of an actual one. The best part of this cardboard cutout was the sticker on the back, something only VHS retailers were supposed to see, not the average consumer. It read, "Your customers will love bringing home 1987's comedy hit, and now you can buy multiple copies for rental for the low price of $125.99 (retailer discount)." One hundred and twenty-five bucks for a video! I had never realized VHS tapes were so expensive. No wonder banks had less security than the first video stores I visited. These places were the Fort Knox of magnetized tape.

Then, *Indiana Jones and the Temple of Doom* changed the game; it was such a big box-office hit that when it came out on VHS, you could buy it for only $19.99! This was thrilling. Twenty dollars was doable. I just hoped the local video store took US savings bonds. But I never had to try, because when my dad picked me up from school on release day, a copy was waiting for me on my seat in his car. It was better than Christmas. I looked at the art and read and reread the description on the back. This was a true treasure. I displayed the lone VHS tape in my room like a priceless heirloom. It was the first movie in my collection. The start of my own video store.

My addiction had begun, and it grew. Because a *Temple of Doom* situation was rare, I did something more grassroots to expand my collection. You could buy blank VHS tapes; those were cheap. So I started making my own rentals. I'd sit with a yellow highlighter and *TV Guide* to see what was playing on all the channels. I began taping movies and TV shows and painstakingly cutting out commercials, which meant using my best instincts and sitting only about an inch away from the TV so that I could hit pause on the VHS machine at the exact right moment when the screen went to black before it went to commercial and then hit play again at the end of the commercial break. My collection kept growing, and my home video store was looking good. Then, with the advent of pay-per-view, I'd rent and record the latest films; that's when I took my store public and I started my rental business at school. Why go to the video store when you could come to me?

It began with classmates; no money was exchanged, but snacks and video game loans were in play. I had a strict one-night policy. Then, my teachers started finding out about my service, and instead of stopping me, they wanted in on the rentals. It felt scandalous, like I had crossed a line, but instead of anything inappropriate going on, they would hold me back after class to ask about getting Tom Hank's *Dragnet* for the weekend.

Since I lent movies to my teachers, they always let me pick the films for class movie day. I started having some genuine power: I was controlling the school's entertainment. I was a middle school movie mogul.

My collection rivaled most video stores, but then Hollywood Video and Blockbuster Video came on the scene. They were the mini-malls of movie rentals. I had just heard tales of these magical places that had plenty of copies of all the new releases and old movies for as far as the eye could see, plus a kids' section and even video games. So when Blockbuster opened in our neighborhood, it was a game changer. When I entered, the bright colors and the rows of videos made me feel like I was in *The Wizard of Oz*. There was no way those mom-and-pop video stores could compete. The weekend our town's Blockbuster opened, if you gave them your other video store membership card, they'd shred it and give you a free rental, in an ultimate corporate *fuck you*. I happily handed over my old card. I know this isn't something I should be proud of, but dammit, I needed more choice, more selection; I didn't understand that corporations weren't my friends—a lesson I still struggle with.

When I heard the cast of *Honey, I Shrunk the Kids* was going to be at my local Blockbuster, I flipped. I dragged my dad down to the store to get in line and meet them. The store was a madhouse; there was a lot of commotion in the kids' section. When the sea of people parted, I saw Amy O'Neill, Jared Rushton, and Robert Oliveri—the titular kids in all their life-size glory. I was handed a flimsy photocopied piece of paper with all three stars' black-and-white headshots on it and was sent by an employee to approach the table for signatures. This was before I made the trip out to Hollywood; I'd never gotten an autograph from anyone other than costumed characters at theme parks. These were real movie stars! I was starstruck and speechless.

I just moved down the line from kid to kid as they each signed my photocopied sheet of paper. (Yes, I still have this signed piece of paper in mint condition, without a single fold or tear, in one of my boxes.) I gave the paper to my dad for safekeeping and then went to look for that night's rental. But I couldn't stop thinking of the kids and how I had missed my chance to impress them. I wanted them to notice me. So I wandered back to the kids' section and loitered off to the side, hoping they would call me to hang out, but they kept signing autographs for their fans. The Blockbuster employee who gave me my first blank autograph sheet of paper gave me another blank one, but before I could tell him I had already met the kids, he pushed me forward to approach again. I didn't protest much, as I was thrilled to get another chance to see the stars up close again and make my move. I was less nervous this time and said, "You were so great in the movie. It must have been scary to be on that giant bee?" I didn't say this to anyone in particular. I just said it out loud to the three of them—a conversation starter for whoever wanted to start a conversation. Instead, they just smiled, signed, and sent me on my way. I never got my answer, but this was my first connection to Hollywood. From that moment on, I knew I wanted to work at a Blockbuster Video.

So about four years later, when I was in high school, my moment finally arrived. I was pacing by my home phone, waiting for Ajay to call me back. And when he did, he said the words I was waiting to hear: "They want to interview you today!"

I ran out of the house like a kid hearing an ice cream truck, jumped into my car, and headed to my destiny. When I pulled into the parking lot, I saw the store and it was giant. It was practically a whole side of a strip mall; it wrapped around the corner.

This wasn't just any Blockbuster store; this was a new model, a flagship store, and I would be one of the new recruits. I walked in and was met by Charlie; he was "Long Island cool," with a Ben-Affleck-meets-CW-star vibe. He had a five-o'clock shadow, and his Blockbuster blue shirt was slightly open, revealing a crisp white tee. He had perfect hair and a great smile. He looked like a ladies' man who was also a dude's bro—someone who played hockey and probably was dating two women and one of them was married. He was everything I was not.

Charlie greeted me and then quickly asked, "You do drugs?" The way he said it, I couldn't figure out whether it was an offer or a condemnation. I was too nervous to lie or appear cool, so I said no. He shook his head and said, "Okay." Then he led me to the stockroom, which was no bigger than a storage closet. It was filled, floor to ceiling, with empty VHS boxes, busted tapes, and receipts. *Wow!* This was cool. In the corner was a small table. He motioned for me to sit down, and as he spoke about the job, I just wanted to pinch myself; I had made it. I was backstage at Blockbuster. Before I knew what was happening, Charlie was approaching me with a pair of scissors. "Put your head down. I gotta do this," he said. I didn't know exactly what he was going to do, but I did as I was told. He then picked up a lock of hair from the back of my head and snipped a sample. "If you are lying about the drugs thing, I'll know; it's all in the hair." He bagged my hair in a small Ziploc bag and went on, "Okay. Ajay says you're cool. Let's see what the drug tests say."

He escorted me out of the break room and asked one final question: "You got a blue shirt and tan pants?" That was the uniform of Blockbuster. I said, "I can get them."

"Good!" He nodded and went back into the back room.

That was it—my first job interview. I knew I didn't do drugs and I had the outfit, so it felt like I had it in the bag. Two days later, I was hired.

Working at Blockbuster was exactly what I had hoped for, and I learned a few things working on the other side of the counter:

★ There was a large and very active crowd of people who were always looking for porn. It didn't matter how family-friendly the store was. Not a shift went by without someone asking where the "adult section" was. I watched multiple people try to enter the bathroom, thinking it was an entrance to an "adult section," only to watch them leave utterly disappointed when they saw the toilet. I got good at suggesting "*Red Shoe Diaries* and some more of our softcore options"—although most people seemed weirded out by my recommendations. I never understood how they could be looking for porn, but when I suggested a viable alternative, *I* was the sex freak.

★ While we are on the topic of adult videos, I know it was a widely held belief that Blockbuster edited content from movies to make them more "family-friendly." But this was just not true; it was the Pizzagate of my generation.

★ When you have access to a laminating machine and work a slow eight-hour shift, you want to laminate everything, and we did. *Note:* Don't laminate your Social Security card; doing that seems to be somewhat illegal, which is something I learned too late, and I'm reminded of it every time I need to produce my card.

★ The best part of working at Blockbuster was the shrink-wrap station. I used that machine constantly for my own personal gain. Since whatever you used it on would look brand-new, the possibilities were endless. Buy a video game at a local GameStop, play it until you're done, re-shrink-wrap it, and return it within thirty days; it looks brand-new, and no one is the wiser. I even shrink-wrapped my own belongings and gave them to other people as birthday or Christmas gifts.

★ You never spoke to a manger. When you called, we would transfer you to a coworker. The manager had no time to listen to your lies about why your videos were returned late. You lie to us; we lie to you.

★ Yes, we did hold all the new releases you wanted in the back until we were done with our shifts or our friends came in. I even tried unsuccessfully to use this practice as a way to flirt; if I saw someone I wanted to talk to looking forlorn that their movie choice was out, I would approach and slip them the new release. Sadly, the difference between doing your job and flirting was hard to parse. When I attempted this move, I didn't know what I expected in return. I'd go up to a girl and ask, "Are you looking for Bruce Willis's *Striking Distance*?" When she nodded, I'd present the copy like a magician: "I thought so." That was it. I had no game, no follow-up. I'd barely start a convo and then walk away. In my mind, she would be so impressed and flattered that I gave her the movie that she would chase after me, thinking, *What else am I missing that this boy could provide? We need to date.* In retrospect, I'm glad I wasn't a creepo, but I also wish I had tried to have a conversation; at least I would have gotten some clarity. Instead, it would just appear as though I was restocking shelves, which was one of my jobs.

★ We kept records of all the jerks. Anyone nasty to the workers had a special note written on their file that only the person ringing up the customer could see. However, after a software update caused those notes to start being printed on the receipts, we got a lot of calls to the manager asking why the receipt said, for example, "Has worst breath." I was known for adding more color to mine, so I apologize to anyone I offended, especially the person who went home with a receipt that read: "Jerks it to Robin Williams's *Flubber*." Thankfully, we did intercept those calls to the manager as well. I can't tell you how many times I told someone I was going to fire myself.

In my first week at Blockbuster, I was thrown into the fray. The store was in the midst of a fierce competition between employees about who could presell the most copies of the new animated Disney movie, *Aladdin*. This was another one of those rare affordable VHS tapes; the retail price was $29.99, but no one was ever paying thirty bucks for that VHS. So we needed to sell the idea that this was the one chance customers would have to own a piece of Disney history.

Let me explain: Disney famously would have its films available for a short period, and then they would go back into the vault. Once the movie was gone, it was gone. We treated this presale of the *Aladdin* VHS like we were giving customers a secret stock tip.

Owning it was like getting in on the ground floor of the Disney fortune. My go-to was this: "If you bought a copy of *Peter Pan* when it first came out, it would be worth over $200. Did you know that? Just think what *Aladdin* will be worth once it returns to the vault in just a few years."

Was *Peter Pan* worth that much? I don't know, but neither did the customers. A quick check on eBay today shows *Aladdin* VHS tapes going for anywhere from $15.50 to $3,000, which is shocking. Apparently, the idea of VHS tapes becoming very valuable is a complete hoax; Snopes debunked it. But there are still people out there trying to cash in on the lie I might have had a hand in starting years ago.

I hated working the counter; its *Glengarry Glen Ross* nature was too much for me. I was bad at sales. I was a floorman; I needed to be out with the people. That's where the action was. Carrying a fresh batch of rewound VHS tapes back to the shelves was a little like being a god; customers swarmed around you to see what was going back on the shelf and into circulation. You had everyone's attention; when you were a teenager, it was one of the few times adults would do precisely as you said. I was like Immortan Joe giving water to the masses in *Mad Max*. I'd tell people to step back and wait. I loved it.

My Blockbuster was also a celebrity hub. *Is it a hub if you only have two celebrity customers?* Once, while I was restocking shelves, a young girl approached. As soon as I saw her, my jaw dropped. *Holy shit, that's Mathilda from Luc Besson's* Léon: The Professional. I wanted to say something, but I kept my cool and pointed her to the documentary section. I was freaking out. Then I started to second guess myself. *Wait. Is that her? Or does she just look like her?* When she came to the counter to check out, I stood nearby to gawk further as I rewound VHSs. When she left, I ran to the manager area and announced to everyone: "That was the girl from *The Professional.*" People shrugged me off. No one believed me. I commanded the cashier, "Pull up her account!"

The dude working the register was confused. "What?"

"What was that girl's name?"

He looked at the screen. "Natalie . . . Hershlag," he said.

I ran over to the VHS box for the movie. I scanned the back, but no Natalie Hershlag was in the credits, just Natalie Portman. My crew laughed. They were right; I was wrong. It was not the same person.

Hmph! I knew in my gut that I was right. Portman must be a stage name. Now, at this point, I couldn't just google this piece of information—because there was no Google. But I knew: *Hershlag is Portman! Portman is Hershlag!* I was content to bide my time, and when she came back in, I would ask her and I would prove to everyone I was right. I was on high alert for her reappearance and occasionally would check her account to see if she had rented anything. Unfortunately, I missed her when she came in to rent Jeff Bridges's *Fearless. What did it mean?* I watched the movie for clues but found none. Sometimes I'd play *The Professional* on all the monitors in the store, hoping it would work like a siren song. It didn't. I never saw her again. (A quick google while writing this chapter proves me right. Hershlag was Portman. I knew it!)

Our other celebrity customer was Chris Martin. Not Chris Martin, the dude from Coldplay—this was the dude whose stage name was Play, from Kid 'n Play. We rolled out the red carpet for him; we told him that if he wanted a new release to call and we'd hold it for him. Charlie would erase his late fees when he was on duty, and we never did that for anyone. We wanted celebrities to know that if they came in, we'd take care of them. It was VIP all the way.

The rush of Hollywood was intoxicating. Unfortunately, we had exhausted our actual celebrities, so we started to make some up; one of my coworkers had a cute friend who lived in the area. Not knowing how to approach her, I decided that the best way to flirt with her was to tell the coworker, Kelly, that her friend looked like Jami Gertz (*Lost Boys*, *Less than Zero*) and we should set up an autograph signing just like the one I went to as a kid with the cast of *Honey, I Shrunk the Kids*. Once again, my flirting game was overly complex and didn't involve actually flirting, just some odd attention in the hope that she'd be wowed by this weirdo, she'd have to know more, and we'd go out on a date. Kelly agreed to ask her friend, not understanding my full intent but knowing that this would be funny. We waited with bated breath for Kelly to come back for her next shift, and then we asked her what happened. She took a beat almost as if she had forgotten. "Oh yeah, she said no." I was crushed. In retrospect, the idea of a high school girl agreeing to this scheme is ridiculous. Of course she had said no. She had no idea what we were regularly up to in that store. It would be like jumping into Kieślowski's *Red* before watching *Blue* and *White*. You can't do that and expect to "get it." We needed to find another way. What if the autograph session was impromptu, and we created a paparazzi event the next time she came in? Unfortunately, Jami Gertz wasn't in a movie that we could advertise. However, Phoebe Cates was. Close enough? Now, all we had to do was wait until Kelly's friend returned to the store and spring it on her. After a few weeks, that moment happened. As she was shopping, we put our plan into effect. We started a buzz around the store.

"Oh my God! Jami Gertz is here."

"You know, from *Lost Boys!*"

"I think she's doing a signing."

This plan would have worked better at 8:00 p.m. on a Friday; this was like 4:00 p.m. on a Wednesday. The little buzz didn't catch on beyond our crew to the handful of people in the store, but that didn't stop us from rolling out the red carpet for our fake Jami Gertz.

As the fake Jami Gertz was checking out, we made a big show of asking whether she would do an impromptu signing of the poster of her newest film. She said, "I guess?" As I unrolled the poster, we got some onlookers. This was starting to be a bit of a scene.

She signed the poster. We convinced a few people to take a picture with her. My plan for re-creating a celebrity signing experience was in full swing. We made a big deal of her exit and quickly hung up a fake Jami Gertz–autographed Phoebe Cates movie poster in the front window. No one questioned it as it hung there for a month, and I never spoke to the fake Jami Gertz again. I heard she had a boyfriend. I should have asked about that earlier, but it didn't matter; I didn't need a girlfriend when I had Blockbuster.

Secretly, for the whole time I had been working there, I was pulling the heist of the century. One of the best parts of working at Blockbuster was having access to the surplus of VHS cover boxes in the stockroom; I saw them the first day I interviewed. They were the flattened boxes that housed all the VHSs. We had a ton of them because we'd only display a handful of cover boxes for the new releases. So, right from the start, I realized that no one would miss a cover box of a new release. By this time, I had two VCRs and was making my dubs, so I'd rent a movie, dub it, and then slip it into a new cover box. Finally my home video store started to look like an actual video store. There were still a few VHS tapes in my collection rocking handwritten labels, and I vowed to get a cover box of every movie I had a dub of. Just like *The Little Mermaid*, I wanted my collection to be complete, and yes, just like my flirting style, this desire was equally complex and hard to explain. But I was in too deep. It wasn't going to be easy. There were cameras all over the store, but luckily for me, I knew where they were, and the security cameras in the stockroom had a nice blind spot, which allowed me to dig through every cover box when I was on my breaks. I lived in fear of someone catching me, but even if they did, it wouldn't be something anyone would truly understand: *So you aren't stealing the thing that's valuable—you're stealing the box it comes in?* I went from getting a cover box every few weeks to getting two per shift and putting cover boxes in the small of my back when I left the store. My manager once noticed a few missing cover boxes in the store; she asked me to look for them in the back, not knowing she was talking to the thief. When I returned and said I couldn't find them, she just shrugged and told me to file a missing-cover-box report, and corporate would send a replacement. *Haha!* I had gamed the system, and no one was the wiser. I finally completed my collection, and I had the ultimate VHS store in my house.

And then DVDs came out.

CLASS ACT

"Your thing is bowling shirts."

My ears perked up. "Yes!" I nodded in agreement as if this were the key to some larger life riddle that I had spent years trying to solve. I quickly scribbled in my notebook, "Buy bowling shirts! It's my *thing*!"

A renowned acting teacher gave me this note and fashion tip. She told us tips like these would take us from being actors who wanted a part to actors who were undeniable in a part. For others she prescribed "fuck-me pumps" or wearing "nerd glasses," but for me, my undeniability was centered around wearing bowling shirts. Could this be the key to success in this business? At that moment, I thought so.

As I returned to my seat, she stopped me. "Wait." She eyed me up and down, and added, ". . . with dress shoes."

This was the type of wisdom I devoured when I took acting classes—something I started doing at a very early age. My first class was at an acting studio run out of a woman's house in suburban Long Island. I was twelve years old, and I wanted to be on *Saturday Night Live*. I didn't know where to begin. I had written to Steve Martin, Bill Murray, and Eddie Murphy. Steve Martin was the only one who sent a signed photo in response, but even he didn't answer any of my questions. So I was out of options. Then I came across a lead in *Newsday*, the local Long Island newspaper, which had a section called "Kidsday": a half page devoted to a local kids' interest story. The writers for the section covered special events at the museum and would write puff pieces on local spelling bee champions, who thought they were so smart 'cause they knew how to spell *nauseous*. I hated those cocky spelling bee champs. One day, the paper printed an interview with a local acting teacher.

Lillian Caron bore an appearance similar to Marlon Brando if he was impersonating Shelley Winters. Lillian had been teaching acting to Long Island's youth from her home for more than a decade. She was pictured in a housecoat, using her fingers to conduct teens who stood in a line like they were in an orchestra. In the article, she refused to name any of her graduates, "out of privacy," but she alluded to the fact that many had gone on to do "great things." Her background was also a bit of a mystery. She had been an actress for many years, but when pressed for details, she simply said she had "too many projects to name." She had now devoted herself to teaching. I called the number listed and begged to take a class, even before I had asked my parents if they would let me. She told me she didn't accept "cold calls" but was going to make an exception for me because I had shown a "true passion." Thankfully, my parents agreed, and when it came time for my first class, my stomach was in knots. My dad dropped me off in front of her house; normally he would walk me inside to whatever class I was taking, but in this class, parents were *not* allowed inside.

As I entered a TV room turned "acting studio," I took it all in. There were kids of all ages running lines in the corner, playing scales at the piano, and even rehearsing stage combat in the center of the room. It was a mini Juilliard, with much thicker Long Island accents and a large fish tank in the corner. Seeing everyone in motion clued me in that while this was my first day, these other students were regulars. I felt out of place. Lillian entered the space like a grande dame, wearing a floral housecoat similar to the one she had been wearing when she was photographed for the paper. The housecoat flowed behind her as she moved, like she was on roller skates. "Let's begin, children," she said. The students all lined up against the wall. I followed. It was an acting roll call. She walked up and down the line, telling us what we would be doing in today's class. She was soft-spoken but articulated every syllable. She made intense eye contact with every person, and every thought was weighted, as if she were parting with a prized possession. She introduced me to the class by saying, "Welcome home." This approach is the absolute epitome of things that give me the willies nowadays, but back then, I was hooked. It felt real. I was in an acting class. It also became very clear that I was the least professional kid in the room. These kids had agents. Some were in soap operas and commercials. They called adults by their first names and scoffed at my want to be on *SNL*. I had a lot of catching up to do.

I didn't have a monologue ready, which caused a bit of stifled laughter from the other students. So Lillian called me over during a scene that was not going well and whispered in my ear, "Go into this scene and do something interesting, but don't say a word." Having had no experience ever performing, I didn't understand the gravity of what she asked me to do: she sent me in to disrupt the other actors onstage. So I walked into the scene as a juggler while the two actors were performing a breakup scene in a park. I was starting to get laughs. I don't think I was doing anything particularly funny, but the juxtaposition made everyone laugh, and it derailed the entire scene. The students got flustered and stopped their scene, but Lillian admonished them: "Paul didn't say a word. You need to steal the focus back by acting!" From that moment forward, she continually used me as this agent of chaos. Instead of performing a written monologue, she had me make one up. She would have me do scenes in gibberish while focusing only on emotion. I quickly became confident being onstage and holding my own with the others.

After a few weeks passed, we got word that there would be a Summer Showcase, and that day she would be giving out parts. The showcase was a lot of group scenes that felt like longer wordplay limericks rather than scenes.

The Interview

#1

Name, please?

#2

Jack Smith.

#1

Jack what Smith?

#2

I beg your pardon?

#1

Fill in the blank space, please.
Jack blank Smith.

#2

Oh, I haven't got one.

#1

No middle name. How bizarre.

Confused? Me too. I still don't understand this at all, and I watched the video of the performance five times in a row while transcribing this opening bit. But I must have been good, because in the next showcase, I got a real scene. This was a big deal. I was cast as a fifty-three-year-old Brooklyn pickpocket, a Willy Loman of crime, who was depressed that his son (who was played by a kid older than me) was more interested in playing the violin than using a tommy gun. In this scene, I did it all: I had a monologue, I had jokes, and I even got angry, which translated into me stiltedly standing up, raising my hands up to the heavens, walking to my mark one foot away, and then immediately returning to my chair. The scene crushed.

After the show, Lillian informed me that her friend who saw the show was casting a new project in NYC and wanted me for a part. I guess she was looking for that rare thirteen-year-old who could play fifty-three? The audition was on a school day. My parents hesitated to take me out of school. I pleaded, "Just this once!"—a catch-22, of course, because I was essentially promising that even if I was good, I'd never ask to miss school for another audition—but logic be damned. There was no script, a situation I'd already been trained for at Lillian's house. I was told to dress "cool," so my mom, who always loved the challenge of making a costume, put me in an outfit that consisted of ripped jeans and no fewer than three bandannas tied on different parts of my body.

We arrived at the casting office, and I bounded up the stairs, excited to start my new life as an actor, thinking this meeting was just a formality—only to enter a room *packed* with kids who all looked like me, minus a bandanna or two. Later, I would understand this type of audition as a "cattle call." I was so green I thought I had gotten the part, and I hadn't realized I was auditioning for it. I didn't even know what auditioning was. I sat in between my parents and waited for about an hour until my name was called. Then I was brought into a room, and they asked me to pretend to play video games, "but no speaking." They watched intently, and after fifteen seconds they said, "Thank you. We'll be in touch."

A casting director ushered me to the door back into the waiting room, where I passed the next kid sitting in my still-warm seat. That was it. The experience was a mix of being incredibly exciting and an absolute bummer. I replayed my wordless audition over and over in my head. *What could I have done differently?* Every day I came home and played the answering machine, hoping I'd get a call and hear something, but I never heard anything. I was crushed. I felt like a failure. Lillian changed the class schedule, and my parents couldn't make the drop-off anymore. I stopped taking classes and my kid acting dream faded away.

A few years later, when I was a freshman in high school, I found myself alone, standing outside a rehearsal studio on West Seventy-Second Street about to take my second acting class—this one was in improvisation. My dad and I had been going to this improvised comedy show in the city, Chicago City Limits. Each show felt like it was pure magic. You'd see the cast play the same "games," but what happened each night was completely original, based on the audience's suggestions. I loved the show so much that I'd drag my dad to it every weekend and sometimes even back to the late show on the same night. We were regulars, so one of the ticket takers told me about classes; I jumped at the chance to learn to be like these performers. But now the time had arrived, and I was there in the rehearsal studio, once again scared out of my mind.

This wasn't suburban Long Island, this was NYC, and I was still a kid, which meant that while I looked alone, I was not. My dad was close by; he recognized the importance of my showing up to the class without a parent, so he gave me an appropriate amount of freedom, about half a block. From there, he would watch me enter the building, and I would return to that spot when the class ended. It was a perfect plan. As I stood frozen at the door at the base of the stairs, a hand tapped me on the shoulder. The hand belonged to one of the show's stars.

"You know it works better when you open the door, not just stand in front of it."

I laughed. He grabbed the door: "You here for the class?" He was going to be my teacher. I was starstruck. Things were going great until I entered the rehearsal studio and saw that this was a class full of *adults*. There wasn't another kid in sight. I don't think I had ever considered that adults took classes. Now I was standing in a circle with ten of them. We started some get-to-know-you games to playfully introduce ourselves to one another. To my surprise, the people in the class weren't actors, nor did they want to be; they were just doing a fun class to loosen up. I stood shoulder to shoulder with an accountant, a guy who worked for the FBI, and a dentist. As we went around the circle and it got closer and closer to being my turn, I made a decision. I needed to lie and pretend to be an adult, too. I told everyone I was in college and had done some improv in high school, and I thought this would be a fun way to break up my intense school week. I waited for someone to call bullshit, but no one questioned my story. I didn't even have to use my fake ID. Maybe it was my height or that once people turn thirty, all kids look the same age to them—which is something I now know firsthand. Either way, my lie worked, and class began.

Since I was with adults, I consciously moved away from anything that I deemed high school specific. Plus most of the suggestions we used put us in offices, at therapy, and driving cars—all things I had no experience with. I just agreed to whatever was said, and whenever I made a choice that didn't work, it played like a joke. The class had a great vibe, and everyone wanted to keep the hangout going after class. This posed a problem. I could keep up the lie in class, but it got trickier in the real world—I didn't know how to do it when my dad was standing a mere fifty feet away from the studio's entrance. I told my dad my situation, eliminating the lies about my age and focusing on the post-class hangout and how it might be awkward to have a dad hang around all these adults.

We figured out a plan. We agreed that adding sixty minutes to the time we'd set aside for class would give me some extra time to hang out, but then when it was over, I'd meet him at a predetermined location far enough away that I wouldn't be spotted with my dad. The class hangouts were fun. Normally we would just go to a diner for a late lunch. But one beautiful spring day, we decided we all needed to go and hang out in Central Park. This posed a problem for two reasons: the park was far away, so now my extra hour needed to accommodate travel time; and I didn't know the city, so even though I might be able to get to the park, I didn't know exactly how to get back. I didn't understand the city's grid layout, and I was nearsighted (and refused to get glasses), so reading street signs was also an issue. But this was the final class hang-out and I couldn't miss it.

As we walked across town, my palms were sweaty. I started making mental notes of places we passed, so I could find my way home. If I had had breadcrumbs like Hansel and Gretel, I would have used them. But as we walked, I got very distracted when one of the students pulled out a joint and started smoking. Once again my sheltered youth kicked in; I had never seen anyone do drugs, ever. My childhood was full of Nancy Reagan and Mr. T telling me to "Just Say No" and watching my drug-addled brain be personified by a fried egg in a PSA. So to see someone pull out "drugs" so cav-alierly and smoke them, in public, in broad daylight, shocked me to my core. I felt like an accomplice in an illegal activity. My mind was racing: *Is this student a drug addict? Will I come home smelling of drugs?* I was completely beside myself. The man started passing the joint to the other members of the class, each of whom took a hit. When it came to me, I did the only thing I knew to do—just say no.

"Nah, I have a baptism I have to go to."

I don't know why those words, in that order, came out of my mouth. But it worked. No one forced me to get high, which is how I imagined drugs were done. We made it to the park, but before I could even hang out, I had to get back to my dad. As I left the group and attempted to return to back to the preestablished meeting point, I saw my dad. He had been tailing us. I don't think he saw the weed because we never spoke of it, but I was relieved to leave this adult world and be a kid again, and most importantly not have to find my way back alone. My Level 1 classmates wanted to continue on to Level 2 together but it was a weeknight class, which I couldn't do. So I told them I was doing a semester abroad. So once again, I stopped taking classes and acting was put on hold.

These classes didn't radically alter my life in the moment, like I had hoped, but they gave me faith that I was on the right track. My teachers and classmates believed in me, and even though I didn't know how to be a professional actor, I started getting closer. As a matter of fact, the first acting job I ever booked, I wore a bowling shirt to the audition. Good thing I took notes.

WHEN I GROW UP

When I was a kid, if any adult asked me what I wanted to be when I grew up, I would proudly announce that I wanted to be on *Saturday Night Live*. The reply was often a gentle laugh and a follow-up: "No, really?" I'd stand firm, and inevitably they would suggest alternative careers: "Ever thought about being a lawyer instead? It's kinda like acting but it pays better." A priest at my school even tried to recruit me to one of the ordained by telling me, "When you're a priest, you play to packed houses every week." The adults in my life were always redirecting me, like offering a dog a toy after you catch him chewing on your shoe. Meanwhile my friends never fielded any pushback about being doctors or paleontologists; no one ever questioned their science and math skills, or examined the pay scale of airline pilots; they just patted them on the back and wished them well. Even friends who wanted to play pro sports were given more encouragement than me: "If you put your mind to it, I bet you can do whatever you want." But acting was a nonstarter. At points I was even actively dissuaded from pursuing my dream. My grandma who worked as a receptionist for a local community theater would call me daily to tell me how many headshots they threw away that day. Once she called me with a special message from the actor Judge Reinhold, who was doing a show at her theater: "He told me to tell you, 'Don't do it.'"

I stopped telling people that I wanted to act. I knew what my desire was but I just didn't feel comfortable sharing it. Being an actor felt like a really lonely and hard journey, and deep down I had this sinking fear: maybe they were right; it was unrealistic, but just like my belief in Santa, I was going to stretch it out as long as I could.

The compromise I eventually reached with my parents was that I could pursue acting if I went to college first and had a "fallback career." Since acting was off the table, I had to think seriously about what I wanted to study. After months of feeling completely uninspired and looking for some direction, I finally found it—on the TV. I chose my school and my major based on where Theo Huxtable from the sitcom *The Cosby Show* went. I didn't look at a brochure. I didn't research a damn thing. I didn't even apply to multiple schools. It was NYU or bust. Thankfully, I wasn't a big Denise fan, or I would have been lost trying to find an application to the fictional Hillman College.

Thankfully, I got into NYU. My essay detailing the conversation between Howard Stern, Martin Luther King Jr., Eddie Murphy, and God must have wowed them. But even my parents were confused about my choice of a major. My mom proudly wore an NYU Film hat when she first visited me. I had to explain, "No, I'm not going to the film school; I'm going to the School of Education to be a teacher. Don't you watch *The Cosby Show*?"

In my first year in college, I switched majors to graphic design, mainly because it was what the girl I was dating was majoring in and partly because the head of the department sounded like Jeff Goldblum, which was as close to an acting class as I was going to get. A few months into school, performing had faded from my mind, and my fallback career that I'd picked by happenstance was quickly becoming my actual career.

However, during my freshman year, when my girlfriend suggested that I get a hobby—maybe a sign of our impending doom—I was stuck. What did I like? "Oh yeah, improv!" *I could do that again.* Chicago City Limits (CCL) had experienced some success and upgraded from a church-basement theater to a converted movie theater on the Upper East Side, and I enrolled back in Level 1, this time as an actual college freshman. Something clicked; my passion was reignited. I remembered how much I loved improv and comedy, and knew I needed to be at this theater as much as possible. Within a year, I auditioned and found myself in the CCL touring company. Well, not actually; at first I was an "alternate." But when one of the new hires left after discovering how badly CCL paid, I was pulled up and made an official company member. Money be damned; I had made it. What started as a hobby was now a job; it felt like my dream of doing comedy could be a reality. I was a working actor. Finally, I'd get respect from all those people who told me I couldn't do it, but I often found it hard to explain exactly what I was doing; people's first question would be "What's improv?" So I settled on telling people that I was in an Off-Broadway comedy show. (*Does the intersection of East Sixtieth Street and First Avenue count as Off Broadway?*)

Now that I was an adult and I had a foot in the door, I wasn't going to let this opportunity go like I had so many times before. I committed 100 percent to the touring company. I took all the shitty gigs; I'd do anything to get onstage—even if there wasn't an actual stage. Like when I did a show where our backstage was an apartment kitchen and we performed for a group of twenty-five people in their living room. While the CCL had a lot of improv games, it was primarily a topical musical revue, which was not my strong suit. That didn't stop me from belting out hits like "Saddam, You're Rocking the Boat" or "Windows 95" (sung to the tune of "9 to 5"). As the group's youngest member, my comedic and cultural sensibilities were calibrated slightly differently. My references were different from the rest of the cast members', who were in their late thirties. I remember having to explain what "getting jiggy wit it" meant (sex), and my song parodies were a bit more out of the box than what they were used to. For example, when I wrote an ode to Robert Downey Jr. to the tune of Chumbawamba's "Tubthumping (I Get Knocked Down)": "*I get locked up, I get out again, you ain't ever gonna keep me clean.*" Sure, that might be cringe now, but in my defense, that song was a hit at the time, and Robert Downey Jr. was in a very different part of his career. While that song scored with the audience, the troupe preferred sticking to song parodies that used classic Broadway tunes and attacked larger pop culture topics like olestra and the high price of subway tokens. Within a few years, I had hit my stride at CCL. I was performing all across the country, teaching classes, and understudying the main stage show. Sure, I made some compromises; CCL wasn't a place where anyone was getting discovered. No one had an agent or was working professionally in TV and movies, but I was getting paid to perform. Technically, I was making it; take that Judge Reinhold.

So when I went with a few friends from CCL to check out this new improv show downtown, I doubted it could be better than what I was doing at bar mitzvahs and on college campuses across the country. But I was open to checking it out.

We arrived at the theater's address, but there was no sign of a theater—just a run-down building with an old industrial hardware store on the first floor. So after wandering back and forth for a while, like first-year Hogwarts students searching for Platform 9¾ at King's Cross station, we gave up. We assumed we had somehow messed up the address and decided to call it quits, which was something that happened a lot before Google Maps.

Just as we were leaving, a tall guy about our age approached us. "You here for the show?"

"Yeah," we replied. There was a pause.

"Upstairs!"

He pressed the intercom button at the entrance to what looked like an apartment building, and when it buzzed, he pulled the door open. "Fifth floor—oh, but don't use the elevator; it's broken." The inside of the building was in worse condition than the outside. The building appeared to be completely abandoned. As we climbed the rickety wooden staircase, I wondered, *Who ever heard of a walk-up theater?* It felt like a perfect setup for us all to be murdered.

But when we reached the fifth floor, we heard music and saw people milling around; this was indeed a theater, and I guessed we wouldn't be murdered after all. We grabbed seats in the small space with about twelve other people who came for the show. I was still skeptical and sank into my seat, ready to be unimpressed.

The lights clicked off, plunging us into darkness. Punk music started blasting from the speakers; strobe and house lights flashed with the music. In an instant, the energy in the room changed to something that demanded you sit up.

A distorted voice blasted from the speakers: "*Ladies and gentlemen, the Upright Citizens Brigade.*"

The "UCB 4"—Amy Poehler, Matt Walsh, Ian Roberts, and Matt Besser—charged the stage. "*Welcome to ASSSSCAT!*" As they introduced the show, they were casual but confident, if not downright cocky. They were dressed in ratty tees and jeans and carried beer in their hands. I had never seen anything like this; I came from performing improv for the whole family in slacks and a mandated "shiny" button-down shirt. But that was not the vibe here. This was like seeing a rock show. They took a suggestion of a word—one word. Then they created a forty-five-minute montage of characters and situations that was raw, edgy, weird, and so fucking funny. They took an intermission and then did it again, weaving both halves together and ending the show on this high note that connected themes and characters. My mind was blown; I hadn't seen sketch shows that could do this, let alone a show that was improvised.

After the show, I was shook. *What is this?* This was different from any improv I had ever seen. It was edgy, adult, absurd, and inspiring. This was my first introduction to UCB and long-form improv, which changed the trajectory of my life.

If you need clarification, many academic texts can break down the differences between short-form (CCL) versus long-form (UCB) improv, but here's my attempt. Short-form improv is based on games, short scene structures predetermined before the show, and you improvise within them. You could see the same structure multiple times with different results. Long-form improv is unstructured; the group creates the show as they are doing the show. No two shows will play out the same way. There is more nuance than that, but this is not that book. Suffice it to say that neither is better, and both can be done exceptionally well or poorly.

I went back every Sunday to see *ASSSSCAT*. I was so energized by the UCB style; I finally felt like I was seeing comedy done by my peers, who grew up on the same comedy I watched and loved. I wanted to bring this style of improv to CCL, but people were resistant: "UCB is a flash in the pan. They won't be around in a year." I felt like I had seen a car but CCL was still making me use a horse— and you know how I feel about horses.

When I heard that UCB was offering classes, I signed up without hesitation. It was a blow to my ego to start as a student in Level 1 at UCB when I was teaching Level 1 improv at CCL, but we were required to start with the basics. I sucked it up, jumped in, and allowed myself to be a student again.

My UCB Level 1 graduation show was on the same day as my NYU college graduation, and I wasn't going to miss it. I was looking forward to my class show more than the culmination of my four years of college. I ran across the stage for the NYU graduation, snagged my diploma, took pictures, and then rushed my family through a celebratory lunch before bringing them downtown to this run-down theater and up five flights to see me perform to a half-full audience at the 5:00 p.m. show. Right before we went on, our teacher gathered us up and told us that before we went onstage, we needed to make eye contact with everyone in our group and tell them, "I got your back." It felt silly at first to be so sincere in the moment before we were about to do a comedy show, but something about connecting with everyone grounded me and made me feel supported. I assume that was a day of highs and lows for my folks who, just hours before, had watched me accept a college diploma on the Carnegie Hall stage. Now they were in their finest clothes, watching me do a scene where my character, a waiter, shits his pants in a restaurant and tries to serve it to a patron for dinner. Post-show, I remember the response from my parents being measured. I couldn't help feeling that they connected with the CCL sensibility a bit more than with this one. I'm sure that, to them, this "theater" felt like a step down from the "Off-Broadway" theater where they had watched me before. So whenever I would talk about my career with my folks, I would downplay my UCB involvement, in fear of being told I was pursuing the wrong thing.

I took more classes and was put on the first UCB Improv Team. Then, I was cast in new long-forms with the other students, directed by UCB. Soon, audiences weren't just coming to see UCB; they came to see us, too. I finally felt I was performing with a group of like-minded people who were on the same page and doing something completely different.

I loved long-form improv because it wasn't always about creating jokes; it was more about finding the funny in the scene. In CCL, it could feel competitive onstage, almost like we were dueling with jokes and puns. But when I performed at UCB, everyone worked together for the greater good. We were a team.

The Upright Citizens Brigade quickly outgrew its first theater and got its own space, a former low-end strip club off Seventh Avenue. Converting a strip club into a comedy club would take some work; it was on all of us, and we did it happily alongside the UCB 4. We painted the walls, converted a runway into a proper stage, plunged the toilets, hung lights, and cleaned up so many disgusting things. I was constantly amazed at where you would find used condoms hidden. They were scattered all around this place like gum is placed under seats. I even pulled one out of a wall. But to be fair that wall was very sexy. In retrospect, it made me really appreciate the hygiene of Show World, which had showers in the actual strip club. In a matter of days, we had built a comedy theater and our new home.

The Real Real World was my first big UCB show; it opened with the new theater and played on Saturday nights. This improvised version of MTV's *The Real World* (which was a very big reality show at the time) was a long-form format where the show changed each week, but the characters remained the same.

Early in the rehearsal process, I was told I wouldn't be a character; I'd do onstage directing. My job was to move the show from location to location, call for testimonials, add characters, and edit scenes. If I did my job right, it would feel like you were watching the real MTV show, and the audience wouldn't even know I was there—which was a gut punch. I was crushed: fading into the background might be suitable for a stagehand, but not for an actor. I got to watch all my friends create these fantastic characters, and my only job was to set them up to score. Was this really what I wanted to be doing?

I was still touring with CCL then, but if I wanted to do this show, I'd have to be available every weekend, so I would have to quit. I had a choice: UCB or CCL? I was conflicted. I couldn't tell what was better for me to do as a performer: stay at CCL as one of the senior touring company members and make money, or commit to UCB in a show where I might be creatively on the bench and not get paid. It seemed like the choice was simple: take the money and stage time. But for me the joy I got performing with the crew of people at UCB was so much more exciting. I felt like I was part of a larger comedy community.

While wrestling with this dilemma, fate put me in front of Del Close, the famed improv guru who had taught comedy to everyone from John Belushi to Tina Fey. He had also trained the UCB 4 and was a mentor to the founders of CCL—a true legend of stage, comedy, and improv.

I saw Del sitting in a beach chair in front of a black box theater on the sidewalk. I recognized him instantly. He appeared to be deep in thought, like a homeowner surveying his backyard, only his backyard was the traffic on Melrose Avenue. He had an aura of "don't bother me," and after much deliberating, I did. I always do. More on that later. I needed his advice, but as soon as I mentioned CCL, his eyes lit up before I could finish. He scoffed, "Tell those people at Chicago City Limits to stop performing that horseshit short-form improv. It's done. It's over."

He was then distracted by another person, and I never got to ask my question, but I had my answer, the answer I knew in my heart was correct: my future was at UCB, no matter my role. I left CCL and gave my shiny shirt and tan pants to a performer who was my size, and I never looked back.

The Real Real World was a hit. It was the first student show that took off. The cast had so much fun doing shows together that a few of us formed a new improv and sketch group called Respecto Montalban, which became one of the handful of house teams at the theater. As the theater started to become a place to be, celebrities began popping up in the audience and even onstage. Mike Myers joined Respecto for a show. He was a comedy legend to me, and now he was asking if he could play with us? He had never met us or seen us perform, but we shared a common language of long-form improv, and he seamlessly fit into the group.

At first it was hard to explain this transition from a paying Off-Broadway gig to a nonpaying black box theater comedy club to my parents—especially to my mom—so I tried to win her over by wowing her with the best show we did at the UCB. I'd asked her to *Killgore*, a hugely popular, once-a-year Halloween show that was way more produced than any other show at the theater. It was a perfect way for my mom to experience UCB, or so I thought. My mom excitedly came to the theater dressed nicely and with her friends. She questioned why the theater was covered in plastic tarps, and it suddenly dawned on me: While *Killgore* might have been the best-produced show, it was also hands down the most vulgar, disgusting, and bloody show the UCB staged. This scripted event show was like a horror movie meets an old-school watermelon-smashing Gallagher show, and it was centered around a cannibal eating someone alive onstage and gruesomely killing everyone who visits his house throughout the night. It was extreme and absurd grossout gore. Midway through the show, my mom and her friends were sprayed with blood from a prosthetic dick that was ripped off my friend's body. My mom took it in stride, but since it was her first exposure to the new theater, I think it was hard for her to imagine what a regular show might look like, which probably explained her reluctance to return.

On the other hand, my dad fell right in line. He loved UCB. He was always a permanent fixture at my shows, sitting in the third row against the wall, camera in hand. He was splattered with blood, and I'm pretty sure he saw 90 percent of my friends' naked asses. He was exposed to so much vulgarity but he never showed an ounce of disdain. Instead, he hung out pre- and postshow, knew everyone's names, and complimented people for the wildest bits: "Owen, I loved that Harry Pothead sketch"; "Jackie, that dildo circus routine was hilarious."

We were doing a lot of shows, but we couldn't just rely on our friends and family attending them. We had to figure out ways to get people in the seats. One of the best ways to get attention for your show was to perform in someone else's popular and successful show. This was a very high-risk, high-reward tactic. If you killed, you hoped you might take a bit of their crowd for your own show, but if you bombed, it meant that you not only would not get new audience members but also would burn your bridges with the people putting on the show.

Respecto was asked to perform at *Stella,* one of the coolest comedy shows in NYC, which was hosted by Michael Ian Black, Michael Showalter, and David Wain. They had all appeared on *The State,* which was one of my favorite sketch shows when I was growing up, so we wanted to impress them and do something big. *Stella* performed in a venue next door to the Blue Man Group, the performance art company responsible for Off Broadway's iconic, long-running, family-friendly percussive, interactive show fronted by four aliens who were bald and blue. In our sketch, we were introduced as the Blue Man Group, and during our bit, we would get someone from our group to pretend to be an audience member and then accidentally murder that person backstage. The bit involved costumes, paint, marshmallows, blood, and, most important, a pretaped video piece that tied all the pieces together.

The night of the show, the bit got off to a good start; just the image of us with blue faces, skullcaps, and matching jumpsuits doing a mix of lousy mime got the crowd on our side. But as we got to the video part of the sketch, in which the Blue Men murder the "audience member," nothing happened. Then we heard a meek voice announce, "Sorry, everyone, we are having problems with the projector."

Fuck!

We had just given the audience the setup and didn't have the punch line. To make matters worse, we were already covered in blood to match the video that would never be seen. Also, per the conceit, we couldn't speak! So we ran out onto the stage covered in blood—the audience had no idea why—and announced, "We killed someone!" Then we ran offstage. End of scene. We bombed (hard). That night, we learned a fundamental lesson: when you fail onstage, it's so much worse when you are in heavy face paint. But no matter how many of these experiences we had of eating it, and we had a lot, we were never alone; we were always onstage with our crew, and after a beer or two, we always wound up laughing about whatever had happened and then got ready to do it again the next night.

* * *

When Lorne Michaels, the famed producer of *Saturday Night Live,* asked UCB to assemble a "best of UCB" sketch show, it signaled that we had arrived. We were now on par with the Groundlings and Second City as a place to discover comedy talent; it felt like real opportunities were finally opening up. While we'd all be competing against one another for an audition slot, we approached the show in the same way as we had all the others—as a team. Then we packed the house with every one of our friends, ensuring that every sketch killed in front of Lorne and the rest of the *SNL* producers. We shared focus and let everyone have their moment. Instead of being a pressure cooker environment, the show was fun, but maybe it was too much fun, because weeks passed and we didn't hear anything. Maybe he hated it. Then, I got a call; they wanted me to audition for *Saturday Night Live*. I couldn't believe it. It was a dream come true.

In a short period of time I went from studying graphic design with no acting outlet to getting a chance to audition for the most coveted job in comedy. I also learned on the same call that I was the only person from UCB to be asked to audition. I felt guilty and I was self-conscious. I was asked to audition because of my performance with all of my friends; to be the only one asked made me feel like it was sort of comedy stolen valor. So I decided that I wasn't going to tell anyone. I was going to go at it alone.

For the next two weeks, I worked alone on my material. I was really missing being able to bounce ideas off my crew.

By the time the day of the audition came, I was ready.

I arrived at 30 Rock at 3:00 p.m. and was escorted upstairs to the hallway where the *SNL* cast dressing rooms were. Every door was closed, and I assumed that behind each door was another person just like me, waiting for their shot. Hours passed as I sat in someone else's decorated dressing room, running my audition and occasionally daydreaming that I got the show and this was my dressing room. Every part of being a cast member of the show was so close but so far away. It was one of the most voyeuristic experiences ever, and then it became even more so. In the corner of the room was a TV. I turned it on. As it buzzed to life, the main stage of *SNL* came into view, where someone was doing an impression of

Sean Connery. *That's odd.* Then it dawned on me. *Holy shit!* I had access to a live feed of the auditions that were currently happening onstage! I quickly turned off the TV. Was I supposed to see that? Was that here to psych me out? I think the answer was . . . maybe.

I learned later that these closed-circuit TVs exist in all the dressing rooms at 30 Rock, carrying a live feed of anything that is taping in the building at a given moment.

My nerves were more amped up now, because I could see my competition. I didn't want to get in my head. I had been waiting for hours in this tiny room. I just needed some air. I opened my door, and there was Kevin Hart, who was doing the same thing as me. I didn't know Kevin; back then, he was just like me, trying to get somewhere in his career.

We had some mutual friends, but we didn't know anything about each other besides that we were in the same boat and feeling the weight of the moment. We just needed to see anyone after hours of being so isolated. We shot the shit and laughed, and I calmed down. No sign of competition existed between us, and we were allies in going through one of the longest and most solitary audition gauntlets that ever existed.

Then, a 30 Rock page approached and called Kevin to the studio. I was alone again. I returned to my room and hesitated about watching his set. To avoid feeling too voyeuristic, I turned it on and watched with the sound off; it looked like he had killed. I waited for him to come back to hear all about it, but he never did. Finally, another page knocked on my door and announced that Lorne and crew had broken for dinner, but I'd be up soon after they returned. A few more hours passed, and then it was time.

It was about 8:30 when we walked from my dressing room down a flight of stairs onto the eighth floor, the home of *SNL*. I walked past pictures of previous casts, looking at faces that defined comedy—people I grew up watching and even some whom I'd recently gotten to perform next to. It felt like I was auditioning not just to be a cast member but to be a part of comedy history.

As I stood outside the double doors that led to the stage, the page said, "You know Amy's in there." Amy Poehler, one of my first long-form teachers and part of the UCB 4, was auditioning for *SNL*, too. The page motioned to the door, signaling me to watch. So I approached the doors and peered through the crack at its center. I couldn't hear anything. I just felt the cold wind of the chilled studio as I saw Amy at a podium doing what looked like a Weekend Update piece. At this point, Amy had already done three seasons of the UCB show on Comedy Central. She was on TV; she was the funniest person I knew. I couldn't believe she had to go through the same gauntlet as the rest of us. I watched until she finished and then stepped back. Amy exited the big doors and, seemingly without any nerves, smiled when she saw me: "Scheer." She gave me a big hug. She said, "It's not that bad—have fun." I couldn't believe how cool, calm, and self-assured she was in the moment or that she was even able to give me advice. She was the first person to know I was auditioning, and she had my back. I needed that. Then I was called to enter the room.

I walked into complete blackness. The only thing illuminated was the iconic stage, where every host has done their monologue for decades. I approached and was quickly surrounded by a team of people. A stage manager showed me the cameras and explained how the audition and screen test would work. A makeup artist touched me up as a sound person wired me. The nerves started to kick in. Then, from the darkness, Lorne Michaels appeared. As a kid who had grown up watching this show, I knew everything about him. It was a magical moment. He was soft-spoken and kind. He asked whether I had everything I needed; I asked for a table, and he snapped into action, calling over a stagehand and requesting the table as if I were the most important person in the room. Once he knew I was good, he nodded, and with a smile, he walked off into the darkness. It was like meeting the president and Santa Claus combined (which, by the way, is an idea I'm developing into a feature film; please don't steal it).

The stage manager reappeared with a clapper, walked before me, and announced my name: "Paul Scheer." The *SNL* logo with my name appeared on all the screens around the darkened empty stage; a countdown happened, and then I was *live* on the center stage at *SNL*. There are all these myths about what the audition is like, and it's not worth listing or disputing them, because all of them are somewhat true and partly false and wholly unique. The things I know that are true: It's an intense experience, but it also feels like they just want to find the right person for the show. I think all that stress leading up to getting onstage is to re-create what an actual live show would feel like. *Can you hack it when the pressure is on? Will you freeze?*

I felt good about my audition; the most shocking thing was how quickly it went. When I was done, that was it. There was no *thank you*, no *goodbye*. I was escorted off the stage and back into the darkness; as I exited the double doors, a page was standing with my backpack in her hand. I was guided to an elevator and sent down to the lobby, and I was back to my normal life once again, probably less than fifteen minutes after my audition started. A moment of utter disbelief kicked in. Then my mind just started to race. *Did that just happen? Was it good? Holy shit, I just auditioned for* SNL. *I hope I get it. I won't get it. When will I know?* I checked my phone, but there were no messages asking, "How'd it go?" because no one knew what I had just done. An existential dread crept over me; my future hung in the balance. Just as I was about to step on an uptown train and head to my apartment, I turned on a dime, ran across the track, and went downtown to UCB.

I walked backstage at UCB, saw some friends, and revealed I had just auditioned for *SNL.* They all perked up and celebrated. I was embraced, and I answered a million questions as I laid out all the details to see whether there was anything we could read into the experience. Laughing and joking with my friends made me instantly regret not involving this group from the start. The energy and love in the space calmed my post-audition nerves. We decided to celebrate with some drinks; I hung behind for a second to dump my *SNL* audition props into my locker downstairs. As I had a moment of silence, it was the first time I could bask in this accomplishment. No one could take that away from me. Then, from the other side of the wall, I heard, "Out of all the people, I can't believe they picked Paul Scheer." Had I heard that right? I leaned in. I had.

The voice wasn't one of my peers or fellow performers; it was one of my teachers, someone I thought was rooting for me. I listened to him continue to talk shit about me, and I just froze.

I didn't know what to do. If I confronted him, it would just be embarrassing. I couldn't see that playing out in a way that would make me feel good. Then I realized that if he found me, it would be even more embarrassing. To make things even more complicated, there was only one way in and out of this basement area, and it was in the part of the basement he was in. I was trapped. So I did what I do best: I hid in an abandoned stairwell and waited for him to leave.

As I hid in my "box," my mind raced. It wasn't that I hadn't heard anyone talk shit about me before. I had. This was different; his status at the theater and what he said played directly into my insecurities. I felt like if I didn't get *SNL*, then maybe this guy was right. If he was right, maybe I shouldn't be doing any of this. But why was I pinning all my self-worth on the outcome of an audition and what someone thought about me? Shouldn't I be focused on the accomplishment and what I had achieved and the joy that I felt in seeing friends and sharing my success with them? Wasn't that the feeling I should be embracing in this moment? Instead, I was hiding from a person who I didn't want to make feel awkward, putting his feelings in front of my own, while my friends waited for me to celebrate with them. What was I doing? For my entire childhood I hid from a mean adult. I didn't have to do that anymore.

I knew I couldn't let another minute pass. I emerged from my hiding spot and walked right into the room where that guy was still chatting it up, and I now saw him differently. I had dealt with versions of this type of person my entire life. He used his power to make people feel small so he could seem big. I used to gravitate toward that type of personality, seeking their validation over others because it was harder won and I felt like it meant more. But being at UCB, I discovered I thrived so much more when I surrounded myself with people who didn't withhold their validation, who told me "you can" instead of "you can't," and supported me no matter what I did. Which was exactly what I planned on doing. I politely nodded my head hello and headed to see my friends.

At the bar I sat with my friends, drinking, laughing, and celebrating this accomplishment. I wasn't thinking about what was next; I was just enjoying the now. I was basking in the fact that I went from a life where I often played by myself and acted out scenes alone to being surrounded by some of the funniest and most talented performers ever. I would never be alone in that way again unless I needed a vanity project. Whether or not I got *SNL* wasn't important. Auditions and gigs will come and go, but in a career as hard as this, the most important thing is having people who will get your back on and off the stage. They always did and always will.

BODY JOBS

Making ends meet in my twenties was difficult. I graduated from college with a degree for a career that I didn't intend to pursue. I didn't want to commit to any actual "real job" because as an actor I needed to be ready at a moment's notice to get up and go if I booked a part, which was highly unlikely as I was barely getting auditions. But I needed to prepare for the job I wanted, not the one I had. Traditional gigs like waitering were elusive because I had no experience (in retrospect, I should have lied). I couldn't get a temp job because I couldn't type (I did lie, but there was an actual test, and I couldn't pass it).

I applied for positions at movie theaters, bookstores, and fast-food restaurants, but I might have been too honest in the interviews. I once told an AMC manager, "I really want this job so I can see movies for free." That statement, oddly, didn't seal the deal. Whenever job interviewers asked me about myself, I wasn't afraid to mention that I was an actor and had a lot of conflicts: "I can't work Monday nights because I have an improv show, and I can't work Friday nights or weekends because I'm on the road with that same improv group." I mistakenly believed these managers would be psyched to be working with someone who did "improv comedy"—they were not.

I also treated my high school job at Blockbuster Video like I was coming from a Fortune 500 company. I bragged to a Barnes & Noble manager, "I essentially managed a Blockbuster Video for three years." The manager looked at me and said, "Essentially?! So did you manage a Blockbuster Video?" To which I replied, "No."

I was always waiting for a follow-up call, but when I hit play on my answering machine, I only received messages for Mikhail Baryshnikov. I'll explain: my home phone was his old number and I guess he didn't tell many people he had changed it because I had a lot of Russians calling me at all hours of the day and once even Barbra Streisand left a message. But none of that helped me. I needed work, and that's when a friend clued me in to "body jobs." Body jobs are jobs that don't require any real skill set; you just need to have a body and show up. An example would be a job as a sign spinner. These jobs always came to me the same way. I'd get a call from a friend or a friend of a friend with a question: "Are you doing anything tomorrow morning?" Inevitably, the answer was no. I would then be given an address and told to show up there the next day with whatever sort of item the job required me to bring along. These were easy money gigs. They often paid in cash, and you never knew what you'd get. I once got paid $500 to walk in a group across the stage at Carnegie Hall dressed in a wrestling onesie and lucha libre mask as the president of CBS encouraged a sold-out crowd of ad executives to boo us—making the point that his network didn't need wrestling to get good ratings. It was the easiest money I ever made. But occasionally, the jobs were a little harder.

"You Rollerblade, right?" a friend of a friend asked one day.

"Of course," I responded, which was an out-and-out lie. I *owned* Rollerblades, but I hadn't mastered them. Who was I fooling? I barely ever used them. In the late '90s in NYC, everyone seemed to have a pair; whether you could actually skate was beside the point. But this was a body job; how hard could it be? The next morning, I grabbed my blades from the back of my closet, blew off the dust bunnies, and headed to a hotel in Midtown for a day of work. As I sat in a conference room with a group of other Rollerbladers, we were told we were very lucky because today we were to be *human billboards*! *Hmph!* The company would attach first-gen LED TVs to our chests, and we would Rollerblade around NYC, "getting consumers' attention" and handing out CD-ROMS for America Online, an old-school web portal that was losing its dominance in the market. When we asked why, we were told, "We create scenes that connect the product to something super cool that people have never seen before." This was corporate guerrilla marketing at its finest!

The shift was eight hours, which was about eight times longer than I had ever spent on Rollerblades. That was a scary proposition, *but* we were getting paid twenty dollars an hour, so it all balanced out. As the organizers tied the TVs to our torsos, we were each given a map of New York City that outlined the spots we needed to hit at certain times (and yes, supervisors would be dispatched to areas on our routes to make sure we were not slacking). Then they placed a backpack full of CD-ROMS on our backs. So now I was balancing what I conservatively estimated to be thirty extra pounds precariously placed on my body, and I was on wheels. The deck was already stacked against me, and then they added the kicker: we were responsible for the TVs if we fell or if they were damaged in any way. So I could lose money on this gig. But I was broke, and this *Squid Game*–style challenge was something I was willing to take a chance on.

The rest of the team took off like they were in a Red Bull ad. I slowly pushed away, grabbing no fewer than seven objects on the way down the block to help balance me. *What had I gotten myself into?* But it was too late to stop now. So I needed to adapt. They wanted us to blade just in the street, but that wasn't happening. I stayed on the sidewalk and made everything in NYC into a railing. I gripped hard anything that was bolted down, and slowly but surely, I started to make some progress. When I got to my assigned spot, I'd just stay in one place, leaning against a wall passing out as many CD-ROMS as I could. I thought if I passed out all the CDs, I'd lighten the load, but at one stop I was met by a supervisor who excitedly refilled my bag—and because I had handed out so many, he gave me more this time.

Somehow I managed not to fall, but that doesn't mean I didn't make other people fall as I was moving down the street, slightly out of control. For the most part, people avoided me as I bounced off walls, bobbling or veering left or right as I bladed down the sidewalks of Midtown. As my eight-hour shift was coming to a close, I was getting a bit better on my wheels, speeding through the city. But as I tried to lift my foot from the crosswalk to the sidewalk, my blades went out from under me. I was falling, and I didn't know what to do; my only thought was *save the TV!* So I tried to turn to fall on my backpack side, but as I did so, the TV became a flying wall that clocked an older woman in the chest, knocking her over. Now, we were both falling in the same direction. If I wrecked a TV *and* a woman, I'd never be able to pay that off.

But then instead of falling, I became airborne! A larger man had seen the crash and lifted me straight up by my backpack. He steadied me on my wheeled feet, and in doing so he gave me a push forward out of the melee. Unfortunately, the woman wasn't so lucky; she fell hard, but I was afraid to stop and cause the same scene again. So I kept going. I screamed back, "Sorry!" and heard in response, "*Fuck AOL!*" So . . . job well done? I made a scene and got attention for the product. Guerrilla marketing at its finest!

There were only so many body jobs I could get, and I wasn't making ends meet.

Thankfully, a friend's mom took pity on me. She recommended me for an open position in accounts payable at a brand consulting firm. I'm terrible at math, so the idea of doing a job that relied solely on accounting was a bit terrifying, but it paid fifteen dollars an hour, and that math I could do. I was going to be *rich*!

The office was downtown, in SoHo. Everyone there seemed

to be living the lives of people that most of us saw only on the covers of fashion magazines or *Sex and the City* episodes. Walking through that crowd of people drinking espressos and perusing art galleries was intoxicating. I arrived at Parker Brand Consulting in the only suit I had, which was wool, and after a subway ride and navigating the streets in the middle of summer, I was in a full-body sweat. Plus I was nervous; I couldn't blow this. The money was too good. I had failed at every job interview, and I was intent on saying whatever was necessary to get this job. I even brought a calculator just in case they asked me to do some quick math. Entering Parker was like stepping onto a movie set; everything was mahogany and brass, and multiple receptionists manned the front desk. I was given a bottle of water and told to wait in a beautiful Eames chair. I was then escorted into my potential new boss's office by his assistant and given a new bottle of water. This was the life. My interviewer had a big smile and a very manicured beard. He had a hip casual look where it didn't look like he was trying but you knew every item of clothing he wore was more expensive than my rent. The detail that was most memorable was that his jeans were so tight that you could literally see his dick. This is something I've never noticed on anyone else before or after, so please take that to mean it was really noticeable.

"So you are a comedian? Tell me a joke!" Please note: never say this to anyone in comedy. There is no good response. Any joke you tell is bound to fail in such a firing-squad environment. As I started to explain, "I'm not that type of comedian," he pulled back: "Okay, okay. Don't worry about it. You're off the hook." I was relieved and then once again got distracted by what was going on in those pants. I was trying to understand where the frank ended and the beans began when he blurted out, "Wanna job?"—to which I replied, stunned, "Uh, yes." And that was it. He called in his assistant and I was hired. As I was leaving his office, he called out, "Lose the suit. We have fun here." It was the first interview that I nailed, and I had barely said anything. Lesson learned.

His assistant walked me downstairs and across the street to a satellite building. It wasn't as impressive as the other space. No lobby, no receptionist, no mood lighting. It was just a regular badly lit office. The company wasted no money on this division; the desks were so close together, it was like we were in a desk warehouse. The employees weren't hip or fashionable. It became very clear we were the ugly part of this very sexy company. The assistant showed me to an empty desk, and I sat down. "Welcome to Parker," she said. I didn't expect the hiring to be that immediate. I asked the assistant, "Should I be doing something?" She shrugged and said, "Someone will tell you." But no one ever did. Not that day. Not the next. Literally months went by, and I was in the office, but I had no purpose. I was like an appendix in the human body or Rocky from *PAW Patrol*.

People were hired and fired, and I just sat at my desk, which had a computer but no internet. But before I could fix that, my computer was taken away, and I was left at just an empty desk. I felt naked but tried my hardest to seem as though I had a task. I perfected the art of looking busy. I made my own tasks for myself, like drawing a map of the United States and trying to learn every capital. I wrote stories by circling and connecting random words in the newspaper. I also used this time for self-improvement like when I spent one week trying not to use the word *awesome* because it upset another coworker.

I also would volunteer to take the mail across the street, just to get another look at the pretty people. My job really took a turn for the worse when a new employee was hired and they took my desk. Now I was just left with a rolling chair—a clear sign things weren't going well, or were they? I didn't know; no one ever spoke to me. I managed to convince another employee to let me keep my bag under his desk during the day, and I hid all my other supplies around the office. I just rolled around the floor all day trying to offer my services to the rest of the staff, which no one ever took me up on. The most exciting part of my day was leaving for lunch, because it was the only time I didn't have to pretend to be doing anything. I even started taking two-hour lunch breaks, because no one seemed to care.

Finally, one day I was actually given something to do. This was an entertainment and branding company tasked with matching products to movies and celebrities, so it wasn't uncommon that celebrities would come into the office (the other office, not ours). However, our accounting office was right next to the photo studio, and occasionally, someone would come in and tell us not to leave our office while the models entered and exited the studio. I guess they didn't want us to scare the models, but that was about all the interaction we had. One day, one of the photographer's assistants popped in and said, "Send over that young guy."

What?! That was me. It had to be. I think I was the only person on sight you would qualify as young in our office, so I walked over to the photo studio, which was bustling with the hippest people I had ever seen. It was the equivalent of going from black-and-white to Technicolor. *This is what has been happening over here the whole time?!* This was magic. This was show business. The lights, the makeup artists, the hair stylists, people standing around commercial boards full of photographic inspiration.

The assistant instructed me to sit, and then a beautiful young woman came over. The assistant said, "This is Britney. I think you two are about the same age." We were. The assistant went on, "You two should have lunch 'cause this place is full of adults." The assistant walked away and left me with the star of the photo shoot. We had a stilted but nice conversation over turkey sandwiches. I asked her about being a model, and she told me she was actually a singer. She asked me what I did, and I confided, "I don't know." She laughed, not realizing I was being more truthful than charming. After a few minutes, she was whisked away, and I was ushered back to my office as quickly as I had been pulled out of it.

Months later, I was watching MTV when I saw the girl I had a turkey sandwich with! *Holy shit!* The video was really good and the song was ". . . Baby One More Time."

I wrote down her name, Britney Spears. I wanted to make sure I was right, that this was indeed the same girl. So I went back to work the next morning, and I told the guy who stored my bag under his desk that I thought I'd had lunch with Britney Spears when she was here for that Tommy Hilfiger campaign a few months ago. Then we did something that was probably illegal. He told me to "check the files." This was Hershlag/Portman all over again. I rolled my chair over to a giant file cabinet, and I found the contract and searched

for the signatures. It was indeed Britney Spears. I stared at the contract that she had signed; she had made a little heart over the *i*. I
needed to memorialize this moment, and if I hadn't already done
something illegal, I was about to risk it again. I photocopied that
document; I don't know why. I guess I just wanted proof. And if
doing that is illegal, I never did that. Also please don't ask to see my
Social Security card either.

After I'd worked there two years, a new boss was hired. Unlike
my first boss, he had an office on our side of the street, and one of
his first orders of business included calling me into his office. He
didn't mince words: "What do you do here?"

I meekly said, "What, uh, what do you mean?"

He continued, "Look, nothing personal, I'm going to have to let
you go."

"You're going to fire me!?" I was indignant. "I have spent the last
two years here waiting and asking for something to do, and no one
said a word. So what I do here is nothing, and as far as I can tell,
that's what I was hired to do. So you can fire me, but I want a six-
month severance package."

He sat there—stunned. I was saving my job by admitting I didn't
have a job. He looked across at me. "Three."

I held my ground. "Six."

"Four."

"Six."

"Five, but you leave right now!"

"I'll take it."

After two years of doing nothing, I got five more months of pay,
and I didn't even have to show up. I was thrilled. True to my word,

PAUL SCHEER

I grabbed my jacket from an empty filing cabinet under the Xerox machine, pulled my bag out from under my officemate's desk, and collected the assorted magazines, DVDs, and pencils I had stored across the office. I stood at the door and loudly announced, "Yes! The rumors are true." My officemates' heads turned. "I've been fired. And believe me when I say, if it can happen to me, it can happen to you! So watch your back!" I held for applause, which never came. Then exited with my head held high.

MY MEET-CUTE

June Diane Raphael and her comedy partner, Casey Wilson, had a hilarious sketch show that everyone at UCB was talking about. It was full of brilliant characters, and their performances were amazing. The show was hilarious, and I instantly became a fan of them both. When Owen Burke, my friend and the artistic director of UCB, asked whether I could help them prep for a prestigious comedy festival, I jumped at the chance. At the time, they were strangers to me, and I was just a fan, so I went back to introduce myself and tell them how much I loved the show. Casey greeted me warmly, and we chatted briefly, but June was a little harder to read. I tried to engage but got nothing. Her attitude wasn't rude so much as it was telegraphing *I don't have time for this chitchat bullshit*—which is a phrase I've often heard her say, so I feel like I read her right. I was immediately intrigued by her. She was beautiful and funny, and I'd be lying if I said I wasn't attracted to her—and not just the way she looked; she had an energy that just felt different from any other woman I had ever met.

The three us up met up a few days later to discuss the show. June was the first to arrive, and I was nervous; she was hilarious, and I wanted her to like me. I didn't know it how it would go, but as soon as I saw her, she gave me a hug—as though we were old friends. I felt at ease, and as we ordered our lunch, a conversation just clicked in, as if we were catching up instead of just getting to know each other. We'd both just gotten out of long-term relationships and were very honest about where we were at. If bittersweetness is an emotion you can exude, we were both doing it; we were excited to be single and out in the world but were also missing our old lives. To this day, we disagree about who was more sad—we both contend it was the other—but for each of us, encountering someone out in the wild who was in the exact same moment created an instant bond. We talked about their sketch show. All I offered were ways to do quick changes more efficiently, because they were the only sketch duo I knew who had costumers backstage assisting them. After lunch, Casey splintered off, and June and I walked for a few more blocks. We said our goodbyes. We didn't make any plans to reconnect. We hadn't exchanged numbers. But I found myself standing there after she left. There was something about her: something special, easy, and sweet. I'd never felt so myself around someone who was still pretty much a stranger.

For the next year and a half, we orbited each other. We didn't run in the same circles, but we had some overlap, so I felt like I saw her at every third party I went to. When I did see her, we'd often soon find ourselves together in a corner with drinks in our hands, and then one of us would be pulled away. And we would have to wait until the next time happenstance would put us together. I finally got her number and was determined to connect to see whether there was something more.

I casually asked her on a movie date; I might even have set it up as "having an extra ticket." She wanted to see *Sideways*, which I didn't think was a great date film, but because she had casually mentioned it, I felt I had to run with it. At this point I'd try anything. I waited outside the theater, and June was late, very late. She texted right at showtime, incredibly apologetic; she had overdone it on a vodka luge at a holiday Christmas party (which is the best excuse ever) and she was taking herself home because she had no business being out and about in the world. I took the cancellation in stride. It wasn't officially a date; remember, I just "had an extra ticket." Plus she had a good reason. So I couldn't be mad. I ended up seeing *Sideways* alone at 11:45 p.m. on a Saturday night, which oddly might have been the ideal way to see that film. In that theater I was essentially a version of Paul Giamatti's character in the film, eating my Twizzlers alone and thinking about what could have been.

After that night, I stopped giving chase. I couldn't really read the situation. More months than normal passed without us seeing each other. Then one night, at a friend's birthday celebration, we saw each other from across a bar; we had barely finished our drinks when we decided to go to another location. We went to Yaffa Café, where we just talked the night away. We would come back to this place a few more times, the same way; time spread out by weeks and months. We would talk as though we had known each other forever but didn't know a thing about each other at the same time. We would sit very comfortably with moments of silence. There was no pressure to define what we were doing; it was flirty but casual. In retrospect, this was probably the best way we could've met; it gave us the chance to get some distance from our breakups and to see other people. It also gave me a chance to work on myself.

After my last breakup, I was becoming acutely aware that in my next relationship, I needed to be different. I didn't like who I was in my relationships; for a long time, I blamed others, but I was starting to realize that the problem was me. Although I couldn't put words to it, the relationships I saw modeled for me as a kid were subconsciously affecting my relationships as an adult.

My parents divorced when I was three, but for a while afterward, they lived together in the same house, acting like they were married. I didn't know then that my dad had moved out and was pretending he still lived at the house. He would leave after I went to sleep and return every morning before I woke up. In my parents' minds, this was the best of both worlds: my parents could be divorced without any of the trauma for me. They kept it up for about three years, while I remained blissfully unaware that anything was wrong. As I grew older, I used to look at this pretense as an incredibly admirable act: "Weren't my parents so selfless?" And they were; I appreciate what they tried to do and how everyone in our lives played along (though I'm guessing that fooling a three-year-old wasn't that hard).

I always tossed off this three-year-long con as a cute side note when talking about my parents' divorce. I'd assure everyone not only that the divorce wasn't that bad but also that my parents had gone to almost unbelievable lengths to make it okay for me. But I have memories lurking below the surface that, whenever I learn some new piece of information, connect to paint a clearer picture of my childhood.

For example, one time when I was little, I woke up late at night, and on my way to my parents' bedroom, I saw a light on in the guest room. We didn't have any guests as far as I knew, so I peeked inside. My dad was asleep in the guest bed with a book across his chest. Why wasn't he reading in his room? I didn't know what to do, so I ran back to my room and pulled the covers over my head, hoping this was some sort of dream and that I'd wake up and everything would be normal again. It almost was; when I got up the next morning, I walked by the guest bedroom and saw that the bed was made. I found my parents making breakfast side by side in the kitchen. Maybe it had been a dream. I remember asking my mom as she drove me to preschool, "Why is Dada sleeping in the guest room?" She looked at me as sweet as could be and told me that their bed was broken so they couldn't both sleep in it. (What a beautiful metaphor for divorce!) I accepted it, no questions asked, the same way I never questioned why my dad was always fully dressed and drinking coffee at the kitchen table at 6:00 a.m., why I never saw him in his pajamas. I didn't want to know the truth—

that he had graduated from the guest room and now was getting up at some ungodly hour back at his apartment to make sure he was at our house when I woke up.

While I know that I was too young to be so clever, I also know that I was too young to be so dumb. I have to believe I was playing my part. Any parent can attest that your kids question you as though you're on trial. I once fell asleep on the couch watching TV late at night. When my sons found me the next morning, they woke me up and asked me so many questions that I started to feel like I had done something wrong.

As a young kid, deep down I knew something was out of whack and didn't push for answers. I didn't want to know the truth. I'd try to get my parents to hug in front of me; I'd pull them together with me in the middle. They'd do it, but everything felt off. We were all lying to each other as we tried to make each other happy.

I get trying to do right by your kid. And I applaud my parents for trying not to subject me to the shock of divorce. In a way, maybe they succeeded; maybe I needed the slow burn of the truth to cushion the blow. I don't remember crying when they told me. I just remember that they were both there waiting for me one morning when I entered the kitchen. I sat down, and they told me they were going to be living in separate places, and the best part was that I'd get to go to both of those places a lot.

They never said, "We're getting a divorce." Nothing negative was said about the arrangement. It was presented as a statement as simple as "We're going to the grocery store this afternoon, and you get to pick out whatever cereal you want." My parents were going to live in two spots; I'd have two bedrooms—and maybe more toys? *Let's do this.* But not "naming" it left a lot unsaid.

The thing that gutted me was losing the house. When I asked what would happen to it, they said, "We're leaving the house, and a new family is going to have it. Isn't that great?!" *No!* I was devastated. That's when the tears started, maybe because it was the most truthful piece of information I had. There was no lie involved, so I could process it, feel the loss. Moving trucks arrived only moments later. As they began to pick up our things, I sat on the floor and stared out the window, realizing that this was the last time I'd sit in our living room. I watched my neighbors hug my parents and the movers divide our furniture into different trucks. I feel as if I went catatonic. I was sad, but they'd told me not to be, so I swallowed those feelings and played along. I dried my tears and tried to put on a smiling face, like everything was going to be fine. I jumped off the stoop the way I always did, one last time, and sat on my front lawn for one final moment. Then I got into my mom's car, and we started this new phase of our lives: Mom and me, and Dad and me—a family forever splintered but pretending we weren't.

As I got older, I began to realize that my parents' three-year charade had created unintended negative consequences for me.

Even though my parents had the best intentions, I do believe at my core that the pretense hampered my ability to trust those I love and those who love me. It gave me a doubt, a belief that all isn't as it seems.

I think this reverberates through my relationships with my parents to this day. That isn't to say that my parents and I lie to one another, but we do polish the truth. We downplay specifics; we "forget" important details in the hope of protecting ourselves and each other. In our triangle, we share information on a need-to-know basis.

My mom will tell me a story ten times, and each time she'll reveal a new piece of information that changes everything. She's a one-person *Rashomon*. Somebody I thought had gone away to college was in jail. Someone who died suddenly had had cancer for five years. You'd think I'd get used to it, but just last year we were having dinner, and I mused, "Where do you think Hunter is now?" I'd meant it as a hypothetical, but she swiftly replied with a city and state.

I was shocked. "How do you know that?"

"Oh, we talked on the phone a few months ago. Pass the pasta, please . . ."

"Wait, what?! You talk on the *phone*?!" She'd *never* mentioned that. It blew my mind. "How do you leave out a detail like that?"

"Well, to be honest, it's none of your business."

I was completely thrown for a loop, but I guess I shouldn't have been surprised, because that was the agreement my mom and I had made about Hunter. He had been such a blight on our family that as we met new people it was easier to never mention him. As a kid, when I asked my mom why we couldn't talk about him, she repeated the same thing she told me over dinner, "It's no one's business." I understand that sentiment, but as I got older, I couldn't reconcile eliminating such a major part of my life from my own narrative.

I kept the secret vigilantly; I think I mentioned Hunter's existence to only three people before I was twenty-one. By that time, I was connecting on a deeper level with friends, and it felt unfair to keep this part of my life secret from them. So I started to talk about it, first with my close friends, then with others. Each time I shared it, I was conflicted. I felt like sharing my story was betraying my mom's narrative, so then I had to lie to her about what people knew about us. For many years, my mom and I played this game of cat and mouse. I was suspicious of everything my mom told me, and I think she was suspicious of everything I told her. We were constantly on our toes trying to suss each other out and determine what was really going on. We were not always right.

My mom once came into New York City to take me out to dinner when I was in college. It was a fun treat—my college eating-out experience was mostly limited to a place called BBQ, which boasted $12.99 plates of "meat" served with enough liquor to make you not taste the meat—but I should have known something was up. She never just popped into the city to get a bite. We met at a fancy restaurant, and I was just settling into a regal-looking chair when she asked, unprompted, "Are you gay?"

I was not. In fact, I was still reeling from a breakup with a woman, which my mom knew well. So I was totally flummoxed. How long had she been thinking I was gay? And it wasn't just the way she asked, but her total disbelief when I told her no. She looked at me like, *What are you hiding?* This was not a casual dinner; it was an interrogation. I was defending myself from accusations of being something I wasn't and, more important, something that I wouldn't be hiding if I actually had been. She kept asking me questions, hoping to crack me, to the point that I started to question my own judgment. *Was* I gay and even I didn't know?

And my mom had come prepared with a lot of circumstantial evidence. First, I had broken up with my girlfriend. That was technically true, but you can break up with someone for reasons other than being gay. She presented her second piece of evidence: I had brought my oldest high school buddy—a man—to my birthday dinner a few weeks earlier. She'd told me to bring a friend, and since I didn't have a girlfriend at the time, he seemed to be a solid choice. She was not convinced; if I wasn't gay, she countered, why did we leave together? The truth was that we wanted to get a drink afterward, but she wasn't buying it. Her final and favorite piece of evidence was that I'd asked for a back massager from Sharper Image for Christmas a few years earlier. "What did you want that for?" she asked suspiciously.

"To massage my back?"

No—she knew better. She knew that it was a "gay sex toy." Now I get that a giant back massager could be mistaken for a vibrator, but I don't think Sharper Image was selling giant dildos disguised as back massagers, and I'd never have had the boldness to ask my mom to buy me a sex toy for Christmas anyway. These questions were insane, but clearly she thought that I was lying and that she had to catch me with my guard down. By the time we left that night, I still don't think she believed me—but she also trusted me enough to ask the question.

Now the apple doesn't fall far from the tree. I also can create twisted fantasies about what happens behind closed doors. At one point, for example, I imagined my dad had a second family living in his attic. I collected clues—drawings, shirts—and I made my mom call my dad and casually bring up his second family, while I secretly listened in on the phone to hear the truth. It turned out all the evidence I had found were *my* things I left at his apartment that I'd forgotten about.

On the other hand, my dad is trickier. He doesn't lie so much as he tries to minimize situations. He wants to prevent worrying, so he swears that major things aren't that big of a deal. He presents all important information as an afterthought. He's the Columbo of important information. "Oh, just one more thing—I'm retiring." If my dad made a newspaper, he'd put the lead story on the back page. He buries information or rushes through details so quickly that I have to make him repeat things all the time. For example, surely I didn't hear him casually tell me that he had just gotten out of heart surgery; I hadn't even known he was in the hospital. We once had a whole lunch together and he didn't mention he was engaged until we were saying our goodbyes.

When he's pressed about why he presents information the way he does, he'll say something like "I didn't want you to get upset." It took me a while to realize that *getting upset* meant having any re-action at all. If nothing is a big deal, then any emotional response will seem out of place, and he never has to live with the discom-fort of someone being upset. I think that in my entire time on this planet, I've seen my dad yell fewer than a handful of times. I never know when he's upset. I used to think that was a model I should copy, and I did.

My family's mentality taught me not to insert myself into any-thing, to always keep up appearances and decorum and not really burden anyone with my feelings.

Juggling a delicate balance of half-truths, omissions, and emotional stoicism created a way of being I thought was normal, but I didn't know any other way. I put myself in absurd situations just to avoid conflict. For example, when my college girlfriend was picking me up for a ten-day stay with her and her parents in Florida, she told me at the airport that she wanted to break up with me. She then added, "I would really love it if you didn't tell anyone either." And I replied, "Okay," even though my brain was short-circuiting as we loaded my bags in her car.

She put the final nail in the coffin when she said, "I'm not even sure if I ever loved you. Want to get some barbecue?" I should have had her turn the car around; I could have said, "Hell no!" But I didn't want to be the bad guy, the angry guy, or just someone who rocked the boat.

So I did what any person whose parents pretended to be married for three years would do; I pretended that nothing was wrong to protect her parents' Christmas vacation! I went through my first major breakup while sleeping in the same bed as my ex-girlfriend. And we did it all: held hands, cuddled on the couch, took pictures with Mickey at Disney World. Her dad even asked me whether we planned to get married. I took it all with a smile, as a burning knot in my chest grew tighter and hotter and I died on the inside.

After that relationship, I was intent on not having anyone fall out of love with me again. Clearly, I had done something wrong in my previous relationship, and I just tried to be perfect for whoever I was with. I never got into fights for fear of upsetting the person I was seeing. My self-respect was slowly chipped away, and I didn't know it, because I was wrapped up in someone else's validation. I assumed that no one would like me if they knew me, the real me. So I never really let my guard down for anyone.

Luckily, I started therapy and began to unpack all of this and was finally becoming aware of these patterns I'd fall into. So June was a bit of a test. Could I do things differently? In other words, could I be me? Since my relationship with June started so naturally and from such a vulnerable place, I didn't have to course correct; she saw me as who I was. As I spent more time with her, I began to understand what a real relationship could be like, but were we in a real relationship?

After a long time of not labeling what we were doing, I decided I needed some answers and attempted a real date with June. But I was nervous about it, because after a year of casual friendship, I didn't want to be that creepo who makes a romantic move and ruins the whole thing. I figured I'd just let the night play out and see what happened. Either way, by the end of the night, I felt confident I'd know where we stood.

We were going to meet up for dinner and then go dancing with some friends. Normally my days were pretty free, but that day, of all days, I got a call that I needed to come into work at *Best Week Ever* in the evening; Chyna, the WWE wrestler, was there, and they needed her to tackle me for a sketch. I was nervous that going to work would make me late for my date, but *BWE* was my only source of income, so I made up an elaborate lie to tell my bosses at *BWE* about my parents being in town, saying we had theater tickets and so I needed to get out of this shoot very quickly.

I went to the shoot, where I was tackled by Chyna, which left me a bit concussed. But it was worth it, because the blunt trauma to the head took away my pre-maybe-date nerves and secured me a paycheck to pay for this date. I raced downtown to meet June at Café Gitane, a cute spot in the East Village.

She was already there. I was late. She looked effortlessly beautiful and refined, and I was probably wearing one of those dumb bowling shirts. We sat at a cramped table, our knees happily touching underneath. We were surrounded by couples; it was a civilized hour, and we were getting together under no false pretenses. I remember looking in her eyes and smiling. Finally, after a bunch of late nights and casual meetups, this felt like a date. But the nervousness of a date wasn't there; maybe we had bypassed that. All I knew was that, in that moment, it felt like the whole restaurant had disappeared and it was just the two of us; there was nothing else in the world. She reached out to grab my hand and there we sat, talking.

It was going perfectly until our friends showed up. The vibe had been white wine and couscous, but they came in like Red Bull and vodka and bacon-wrapped street hot dogs. Suddenly, the romantic duo became a foursome, and the dynamic of the date changed. They pulled up chairs from a nearby table; our romantically cramped two-top became an overcrowded four-top. They positioned themselves on either side of us, dividing the table into girls' and boys' sections. Our hands separated as our friends reached over the table to grab leftover bread and apps, avoiding ordering food to save money, and ordering hard liquor instead. Nothing they did would have felt wrong if it had been just a normal meetup with friends, but they inadvertently busted in on my most romantic date ever, and within an instant it was over. Just as June and I connected, we were pulled apart. Was the world telling us something? Maybe we just weren't meant to be. As our friends raged, we shared a look with each other that said, *Damn*. While small, that look made me feel like maybe we were on the same page and all hope wasn't lost.

We downed a quick drink and headed out to dance. I had never been dancing before, but I wanted to because when I was with June, no matter what we did, I was having fun. I quickly realized that an '80s dance club isn't the perfect spot to keep a conversation going. We became two bodies in a sea of sweaty New Yorkers whose movements pushed us together and pulled us apart. We eventually reunited when the dance floor began to thin out, and the connection we had was starting to re-form. We were back in each other's world, and no one else mattered.

Then June excused herself, and I grabbed a last drink for us both at the bar. I felt like this night was going really well, and I finally had some clarity. Then my friend sidled up to me. "She just likes you as a friend," he said.

What?

The two drinks I had ordered landed in front of me. "As a friend" rang in my ears.

In an instant, all the wind was sucked out of my sails. My posture crumpled; my mind was racing. Had June told her friend to tell my friend that I should back off? What did I do wrong? I thought we were connecting. I saw my friend's lips moving, but I couldn't hear anything he was saying. I felt dumb. Did I totally misread this whole situation—and for a whole year? I saw flashbacks of every moment June and I had shared, tinged with this news. Was she lying to me? Was she trying to give me a hint that she wasn't interested all along, and I never got it? Every interaction seemed different now. The realization instantly sobered me up. The one thing I was thankful about was that my friend had told me; he had protected me from having to hear this from June.

I wanted to leave, lick my wounds in solitude, but I went back to my new relationship mantra: *Do it different*. I took a breath and told myself, "Fuck it. It's fine." I liked June, and maybe she didn't like me the way I wanted her to, but why not keep dancing? I was having fun and I liked being with her; if it was as a friend, so be it. I could adjust to that. I just wanted her in my life. I wasn't going to erase this person because I was embarrassed.

But when June came back from the bathroom, she still had a flirty vibe. She was flirting even *more* than she had been before. Weird? But I just went with it. I flirted back. *Do friends flirt? Maybe we are friends who flirt.* That seemed to have been our MO before this night. So I embraced it. Soon it was last call, and our friends were off, leaving us alone in the quiet to get our winter coats from the sticky banquettes, which looked way less appealing with the lights on. It was mid-December, and it should have been freezing so late at night, but it was beautiful outside. I flagged down a cab and offered it to June, but she wanted to walk. *Hmm* . . . so I sent the cab on its way and joined her. She put her arm in mine and we headed east.

The city moved in slow motion around us and we glided through the nearly empty streets. If you'd asked me before the night started how I wanted it to end, I would've said like this.

We got to her place. I remember looking at June's beautiful blue eyes, which looked even brighter on this cold night as we stood motionless in front of the door. There was a pause.

Then she leaned in and kissed me. It had started to snow, and I couldn't even enjoy the magic of the moment, because as soon as our lips touched, I thought, *What the fuck??*

Before I could even process what had just happened, June took off like a bunny. She disappeared into her building. I can't remember whether we said goodbye, but I stood in the street, frozen and utterly confused, replaying the moment. *Maybe it was a friendly kiss? But it was kinda long. Do friends long-kiss? They could. We flirt. Maybe we are flirty, kissing friends.* I didn't know.

I spent the next week replaying the entire night in too much detail to all my friends. I got a lot of conflicting opinions, and June's texts were confusing:

Was she being flirty or blowing me off? This was the time of T9 texting (google it) so it was always harder to tell. After weeks of confusion, endless role-playing with friends, and a few too

181

many tiki drinks at a holiday party, I impulsively (i.e., drunkenly) texted:

Wanna come 2 Party?

Sure.

Seeing "Sure" pop up on my screen sent me into a panic. *Oh no? She's coming. I need a plan.* Then I realized that I was too drunk for a plan. So I was going to wing it. When June entered, as sober as the day is long, I knew this was going to be tougher than I had imagined. I had to be smooth. As she approached, I blurted out, "Do you like me? Because I like you."

Then, in the simplicity of a T9 text, she said, "Yeah." I pulled her in close, and we kissed for the second time. I never wanted to let go. This time was going to be different.

SCHEER HUMILIATIONS

My childhood run-in with Alan Alda was just the beginning of a lifetime of odd interactions with celebrities. The following stories represent a small sampling of traumatic embarrassments.

WAITING FOR THE POLICEMAN

I had a big car, a 1977 Oldsmobile Cutlass, and driving in New York City was always a bit of a nightmare. One afternoon, the traffic was unusually bad, and I was waiting forever in massive gridlock to turn onto Hudson. I was slowly moving my car forward into the intersection, hoping to be able to squeeze in before the next light when a cyclist came flying through the crosswalk. I braked, narrowly avoiding a collision. The cyclist hit his brakes, too, stopping right in front of my car. He got off his bike and took off his helmet; he was pissed. *Oh no, this is going to be bad.* He turned and faced me and slammed his hands down on my hood, giving the car a bounce, looked me dead in the eyes, and screamed, "What the fuck are you doing? Learn how to drive, you piece of shit." I was stunned, not because I was being berated but because I realized the cyclist was Lou Reed. Yes, I almost put the frontman of the Velvet Underground in the ground. He sneered as he jumped back on his bike and rode off. I managed to shout out, "Big fan!" To which he replied, "Asshole!"

HEY, HEY, HEY . . . IT'S A . . . WEIRD DUDE

In the early 1990s, I saw Bill Cosby at a college basketball game at Madison Square Garden. This was back in the day when he was most notable for being the endearing Dr. Huxtable, America's favorite dad . . . I was such a fan of *The Cosby Show.* I was so excited to see him in the real world. I went up to him during a break in the game and said, "Mr. Cosby, can you sign my program?"

Nothing. He didn't move. He didn't acknowledge my presence. He just stared in front of him.

I repeated myself, thinking he hadn't heard me: "Mr. Cosby, can you sign my program?"

Again, he just sat motionless, like someone frozen in time.

I had no idea what was going on. Was Cosby okay? Was he having a stroke? Did I need to call for help? I continued to stand there, not really understanding what was happening. Part of me hoped he was making a joke.

Then he turned his head, meeting my eyes, and like an angry Svengali whispered, "Go!" Then he turned his head back to the game, once again frozen. Chills went up my spine. I immediately went back to my seat and sat down. When my dad asked how it went, all I could muster was a muted, "Bad." And I never talked about it again.

I'VE HAD IT WITH THIS MOTHERFUCKING SCHEER NEAR MY MOTHERFUCKING TRAILER

Samuel L. Jackson was filming *Shaft* in my neighborhood in NYC. I was not only a huge fan of Sam but loved the original *Shaft*, so every day I made it a point to walk by his trailer hoping to catch a glimpse of him. A few days had passed and I had no luck. Then one afternoon I was running an errand and made a quick pass by his trailer, when I saw Sam Jackson, alone, heading to his trailer from the other direction. We made eye contact. A huge smile crossed my face as I saw him. We were about ten feet apart and no one else was around. I wanted to get his autograph, but before I could even open my mouth, he looked me up and down and said, *"Fuck no!"* Was he saying "Fuck no, I won't sign" or was he just cursing my entire existence? The way he said it, I felt like either was valid. I stopped in my tracks, taking in this ultimate rejection as he breezed by me and entered his trailer, slamming the door behind him. I guess Shaft is a bad mother ...

"Shut your mouth!"

"But I'm talking 'bout Sam Jackson giving me the shaft."

KEEPING UP WITH A CARDASSIAN

When I was in high school, I visited Los Angeles by myself. It was a little lonely, but I filled my days the way my dad taught me:

attractions, buffets, and amusement parks. One of my first stops was a tour of the Paramount lot. It supposedly was the best studio tour; Paramount's slogan was something like, "This isn't a theme park; this is a working lot." We were bound to see some celebrities, and I was psyched. As we toured the stages, our guide asked, "Who likes *Star Trek*?" My hand shot up, hoping to grab his attention, but that wasn't an issue because no other hands went up but mine. I loved *Star Trek*, and so did the tour guide. In between the guided parts of the tour, we would walk together, quietly chatting and geeking out about *Trek*. Which was great for me because everyone else was on the tour with family and friends, so I finally had someone to talk to.

We got to a big stage, and the tour guide announced, "Behind these walls, they are filming *Deep Space Nine*."

Then, almost on cue, a door opened, and an actor in full alien prosthetics walked out; our tour guide announced, "Ladies and gentlemen, ███████████ from *Deep Space Nine!*" The tour guide pulled the actor over, and our group pulled out cameras, excited but not overwhelmed—a tough spot for any actor to be in. It was quickly getting awkward and then I made it worse. The tour guide knew this celebrity sighting was floundering, so he threw to me: "You recognize him, right, Paul?" All I needed to say was yes, but in a moment of pure honesty, I excitedly said, "No!" I got a huge laugh from the group. I could instantly tell even behind the many layers of latex that I had offended this actor, which was the last thing I wanted to do. The tour guide stared daggers at me. I tried to recover: "I didn't mean it like that; I think I know him . . .

you. I mean, I want to know you . . . I'm interested . . . in him?" The damage had been done. The actor shrugged it off, pulled out a cigarette, and walked away from our group. As he got out of earshot, the tour guide admonished us: "Just so you know, he's played a lot of roles on the show."

Then he turned to me. "And I thought you said you were a fan." The tour guide took off ahead of the group and didn't talk to me for the rest of the tour. I was all alone once again.

WE COME TO THIS PLACE TO FEEL AWKWARD

I embraced my role as a New Yorker. I lived in a touristy area of the city, so I often had to fight through crowds of rubbernecking people who were taking in the sights and sounds of the area. I would bob, weave, and snake in between them. I felt like I was in a human game of *Frogger* as I got from one street to the next. It was unusually crowded on Fifty-Fifth Street. I was on the phone and lost in the conversation, but as the crowd got thicker, I turned up my normal New Yorker energy and just barreled through what seemed to be a throng of tourists. I finally pushed past a man in a suit trying to stop me, only to come face-to-face with Nicole Kidman, dressed to the nines, as she exited a limo. Flashbulbs were going off. I made eye contact with her shocked face, only at that point realizing that she was just about to walk the red carpet at the Ziegfeld, and I had just barreled into the premiere like a late-arriving date. I panicked. *What did I just do?* So, in an attempt to save face, I exclaimed, "*This is ridiculous!*" gesturing to the assorted fans and paparazzi. Then, without missing a beat,

I kept walking right past her. Somehow my self-righteous anger felt good in a place like that, and thankfully, I wasn't arrested for almost attacking Nicole Kidman.

BASHVILLE

Back in the mid-2000s, *Friday Night Lights* was still in its infancy, and I saw Connie Britton leaving the movies. I was a fan, and I wanted to say something, but I also didn't want to blow her cover in a crowded space or risk making things awkward, so I came up with a plan: I made a beeline toward her and quickly blurted out, "I just want to tell you I think you are phenomenal. Love your work. Have a great night."

As quickly as I said this, I kept walking—it was a gratitude drive-by. While it may have been a bit unnerving in its speed, I was proud of that interaction. I geeked out and got out—perfect.

It felt good until, the following weekend, I went to a wedding where I realized that my friend was dating Connie Britton and we were all seated at the same table. *Fuck!* Now my mind was racing: *Does she realize I'm the same guy?* It was so recent. When she sat down, we shook hands, and she stopped, looking curiously at me. "We've met, right?"

My brain raced through how this could play out. *Do I just admit it? Maybe it will be funny. No, it will be weird.* So I did what I do best in moments like these: I lied. I pretended to think for a second and said, "I don't think so?" I couldn't tell whether she bought it, so I went to plan B: out of sight, out of mind. I literally didn't go back to the table for the rest of the night. I ate at a different table. It was the only way I could be assured not to have an awkward moment. June was confounded: "Where did you go?" To which I replied, "I'll explain later, but just trust me when I tell you I was protecting you . . . from me."

DREAMWEAVER

To know me is to know that I am a huge *Buffy the Vampire Slayer*, *Angel*, and *Firefly* fan. I've been on board since the beginning, and the creator of those shows, Joss Whedon, while now problematic, back then was one of the preeminent voices of pop culture. In 2010, when I was interviewed for a documentary about San Diego Comic-Con, I said my dream person to meet was Joss Whedon. He was the SDCC king; from raucous panels to late-night dance parties, he was everywhere. I had never met him. I had learned from all my previous awkward encounters that it would probably not go well, so better to avoid it. But saying it in a documentary was harmless. The following year I was back at Comic-Con at a big party. I was all alone, waiting for my friends to get past security, when I felt a gentle tap on my shoulder. I turned and was suddenly face-to-face with Joss. "I heard it was your dream to meet me," he said. My jaw dropped. It took me a second to put it all together: the documentary had screened earlier that weekend, and he must have seen it and now he was giving me my chance to live out my dream, but with an introduction like that, I was dead in the water. It felt like the person I had a crush on had read my journal. All the excitement of meeting him fizzled.

How do you have a normal conversation with someone after

they tell you they know they are your dream person? You just can't segue into casual conversation. I couldn't deny having said what I had said, the way I would normally do, because it was on film. So I just really downplayed it: "Oh yeah . . . weird, right?" I still don't know what I was asking him to agree with: that I was weird for saying what I had said or that he would be a weird choice for anyone's dream person. I was floundering, and this already awkward moment was getting worse by the second. "How's your Con?" I blurted out (disgusted by my lame follow-up). Joss, without breaking eye contact, just shrugged off my question and stared at me with the anticipatory look of someone who is waiting for me either to launch into glowing adoration or to ask a burning question. My dream at the time was to work with him, so I didn't want to be a fan; I wanted to be a peer, or at least peer-adjacent. If I geeked here, he'd never hire me. Feeling I was at a stalemate, I quickly hit the conversation eject button: "I'm actually supposed to meet my friends down the street. I'll catch you later?" And I walked away from him and actually left the party! The party I had just arrived at. As I walked out the door, my friends, who had just passed security, looked at me with stunned disbelief. I mouthed, "I have to go!" I went back to my hotel room and sat alone for the rest of the night because that's what I deserved.

Pro tip: Honestly, let this be a lesson for anyone who has an awkward interaction at a party—leave. Nothing is worse than having a weird interaction and staying at the party. The whole rest of the night, every time you catch a glimpse of that person out of the corner of your eye, you go right back to that horrible moment. It's impossible to escape.

THE FRIEND OF YOUR FRIEND IS MY ENEMY

While I was working on a movie, I had become friendly with one of the younger producers on set. A tough-looking dude, he was tatted up and looked like he benched while making deals. Every day we'd sit together in the van driving to set, and he would tell me stories about all the films he'd worked on. He'd gotten his start with Robert Downey Jr. He loved Robert, and I guess the feeling was mutual; he'd worked on a bunch of RDJ's films after *Iron Man*. Also he called Robert "RDJ." Clearly, they were close.

As I wrapped on the film, he asked me whether I was going to San Diego Comic-Con the following weekend. I was. He said something like "If you see RDJ, tell him we're buds. He'd love to meet you." I filed this in my mind as a thing I would not be doing. This was also the first year that I was at Comic-Con with June. I really wanted to show her a good time, because I know a large crowded place full of nerdy stuff isn't really her sweet spot. I had a perfect plan. I was going to give her a backstage experience at one of the coolest events at Comic-Con, Hall H, the biggest room at the Con. My thought was that the uniqueness of the experience would make her an SDCC devotee. Because I had hosted a panel in Hall H earlier in the day, I had a special badge that gave me full access to the convention center. So June and I got some lunch and drinks (and a few more drinks; I think she was delaying her entrance into the venue). We arrived right before the panel started and went into the greenroom, which oddly was a few floors above the convention hall.

A voice called, "Places," and everyone headed to the elevator. I grabbed June's hand, and we joined this giant Marvel group and shuffled to the elevators.

My intent was purely to observe, but somehow I wound up standing right next to RDJ. Those drinks we'd had were dulling my very emphatic "don't meet your idols" policy. The elevator was taking a while to come, and I said, "Hey, Robert."

First of all, *way too casual*! I blame the margarita or maybe that dumb parody we sang about him at CCL. Robert turned, and you could tell that in a room full of people he knew, I was not one of them. "I'm friends with ███████████." *Pause.* I was expecting an immediate smile of recognition, but Robert cocked his head, the way dogs do when they don't understand something.

At this point, June released my hand. She wanted nothing to do with me and walked away backward through the crowd. She oddly had the closer connection to Robert, as she had done a movie with him. Now I was alone. Seconds felt like minutes. I swallowed hard but I pushed forward: "███████████ told me to say hi." Robert looked at me, even more confused, his eyes squinted. I started to sweat. Robert was looking at me as though I was a nut job.

Trying to save face, I started to blurt out a lot of facts about ███████████—things that were so specific, this person couldn't be confused with anyone else. Nothing was ringing a bell. Now it seemed like RDJ's confusion was leading to irritation.

He stopped me and said, "Yeah, I'm sorry, man, I don't know that guy." At this point, his security guards turned toward me. These men were *giant*. They had necks that were bigger than my thighs. My heart was racing. I didn't know what to do; I didn't want to be the weird person in this interaction. So even though RDJ had given me a clear (and kind) end-of-conversation moment, I tried to save face. "I'm sorry, I must have confused you with someone else . . ."

What?! What was I saying? How could I possibly confuse the biggest movie star in the world—*Oh, you know, I actually was thinking of Robert Downey Sr., yeah, yeah, not junior*—with his eighty-plus-year-old *dad*!?

My statement hung in the air. RDJ looked at me: "Oh."

I needed to get out of there. I tried to move but I was stuck in this tight crowd of people. The elevator finally dinged, everyone moved forward but me, and I stood my ground as people pushed past me. There was no way I was getting on that elevator. The doors closed, and I looked at June, who stood a good five feet away, and she asked, "What did you do?" She shook her head in disbelief. Honestly, I had no idea.

A decade later I was on set of *Avengers: Infinity War*. I had some friends in the film, and I was chatting with them when I saw RDJ appear on set. I felt his glare on the back of my head. When I turned, I saw him whisper to someone and point at me. Did he remember that moment? *Oh God, no.* I couldn't take a chance, so I did what I always do: I left. I got out quicker than Tony Stark could snap. Yes, I sacrificed having the biggest fanboy experience of my life to avoid either of us having to relive that moment, and I couldn't have been prouder of myself.

When people say, "Never meet your idols," it's intended as a warning for people who are meeting their idols. But for me, I believe this saying is meant to protect my idols *from me.* In the past few years, the number of big celebrities I've avoided is impressive, and I always sleep better at night knowing I didn't create an awkward core memory for them or me.

WiLL YOU MARRY ME?

Stephani was my sixth-grade girlfriend. She liked the Beastie Boys, wore multiple snap bracelets, and always rocked neon scrunchies. At one point there was talk among Stephani's friends that if I "*liked her liked her,*" I should get her a "Claddagh ring"—which was a middle school way of showing everyone you were "taken." Where would I even get this ring? So I enlisted my mom; this was an assignment she was built for, but I forgot that my mom doesn't do anything simply. "Yes, we need to get a ring, but not a Claddagh ring! Those are ugly." Instead, she brought me to the jewelry section of Macy's that had more traditional-looking engagement rings that were a step up from costume jewelry. These rings meant business. I spent fifty dollars on a very large faux-diamond engagement ring. I was nervous; it was a lot of money, and it seemed a bit adult. My mom blew off my fears: "Women want diamonds." When I presented the ring to Stephani after school, her eyes went wide; she wasn't expecting this. She gave me a huge kiss, slipped it on her finger, and then ran to her bus. My mom was right, which was why I was confused when I never saw her wear the ring again.

I asked her friend Tiffani (*i* names were big in the '80s) why Stephani never wore my ring. She said, "Her parents freaked out." I shrugged it off, not really understanding why. But as an adult I can only imagine the shit show that happened when their eleven-year-old came home with an Elizabeth Taylor–sized ring on her hand. It was completely inappropriate. After that debacle I swore off buying jewelry for anyone and I kept to it until I got engaged.

As a kid, I had a long list of people I wanted to marry, and according to a Magic 8 Ball, Punky Brewster looked "most likely." And sadly, Alyssa Milano was "outlook not so good." But as I got older, I didn't think about marriage at all. There didn't seem to be a reason for it. If you were in a long-term relationship, you could do everything a married couple could, and I was always eager to repeat some reasons that proved my point.

Why do I need a piece of paper to prove I love someone?

We'll only do it if we are having kids.

I'm standing in allyship with my friends who can't get married.

Kurt and Goldie, they never got married, and I think they're happier because of it.

I had a lot of excuses that sounded good enough.

But I had other reasons, too. I'd lived through multiple marriages and divorces; by the time I was thirty, five people had asked me to call them Mom or Dad. The sheen of marriage just didn't appeal to me. Plus I was starting to figure out who I was in a relationship, and it was going really well. Why change anything?

But then something did change. June. We had been together for a few years, and it was getting better and better. Then one morning I woke up with the overwhelming feeling that I wanted to marry June. It was like I had been subconsciously debating the idea, and I finally knew the right answer. All my rational reasons why not went out the window. I knew this was my person and I wanted everyone to know it, too.

But now what?

None of my married friends ever shared how they found a ring or planned their proposals. I only saw the aftermath, a ring finger in my face with the announcement—"We're engaged!"—but the lead-up seemed shrouded in mystery. What was I supposed to be doing? How *do* you get engaged? So I called my good friend Owen; he was married, he had done this, and I asked him, "What do I do?"

His answer was simple: "Get a ring." I listened intently. *Okay, makes sense.*

"How?"

"You go to a jewelry store."

Everything felt so insurmountable; this was something I didn't do. Should I go back to Macy's? How would I know which rings were the good ones? He calmed my fears and anxiety by walking me through every step that he took with his wife for their engagement, and when he was done, I felt like I had a blueprint on how to tackle this. Before I hung up, I asked him one final question, "How do you know it's the right ring?"

"When you see it, you'll know."

I have a tendency to be obsessive, so I went to every ring store in LA (and online), not even knowing what I wanted but trusting the process. I started with some high-end stores and even went to a wedding ring factory warehouse, which was a like a Payless for diamond rings. I drank so many glasses of champagne while I viewed diamonds on felt trays. I even examined dead people's engagement rings (that's a thing). I perfected casually saying "not really my style" when I saw a price tag quadruple what I was expecting. I even designed my own rings online, which always came out horribly. I heard about the three Cs, but whenever I got a diamond lecture, I always made the same face, the one I make when someone gives me directions. I'm actively trying to listen but not remembering a damn thing. I was waiting for the magical moment when I'd see a ring that screamed, "June!"

Then I did. Owen was right. I finally saw June's ring, which was good because at that point I felt like I had seen 98 percent of LA's entire diamond population, and I was getting nervous I'd have to start traveling to different cities. I loved the ring; it had June's personality. June's style is so effortless and classic; she is someone who looks as amazing in a T-shirt and jean shorts as she does in a designer dress. And this ring matched that style. I just hoped she'd love it, too, because all these places had a no-return or a return-at-a-loss policy. This ring was the most expensive thing I had ever bought, beating out a couch from Crate & Barrel; that was $1,200, and buying that stressed me out so much I momentarily questioned if I even needed it—*Maybe I should just sit on the floor.* This ring was more expensive then the couch, but oddly, I didn't have that same anxiety. I was just excited to give it to June and start this next chapter of our life.

So the first part was done. I got the ring.

Now I just had to propose. How was I going to do it? Luckily, for this part I had a plan. I knew I wanted to do something small and personal. I wanted it to be like those first nights we ever spent together, just the two of us. But then: *What do I say? How do I articulate how she makes me feel when I'm around her?* This is always where I completely fall apart. I'm envious of people like June who actually can articulate feeling and emotion so succinctly, so personally. My emotions don't come out perfectly as words. They come out either very analytical or overly obtuse. Very rarely is there an in between.

I just knew this: I loved June unconditionally and I knew she felt the same. In our time together we stood taller beside each other in the darkest of times, and we always found joy in whatever we did. We were honest with each other but never mean, and I looked forward to every day with her. It took me like an hour to write that. *How am I going to say that off the cuff?*

The biggest part of my fear of proposing and articulating myself in that moment was that I was doing this in secret. She wasn't a part of this decision, so I wanted to make her feel like it was something I had really thought about and wasn't doing lightly. But as with any proposal, it would mean fully letting my guard down and opening myself up to the biggest rejection. Especially since we hadn't really talked about marriage—I mean, we talked around it. Our conversations felt like two spies working each other for information and neither of them would break.

PAUL SCHEER

Well, you don't want to.
I didn't say that.
Well, do you?
Do you?
I'm not against it.
Me neither.
But do we need it?
I dunno.

I just didn't want to mess up what we had, but through this whole process, I kept feeling stronger and stronger about my desire to do this, so it was time to put everything on the line. Plus I had bought the ring, so there was no turning back.

I waited till the last second to call her dad, John. He was horrible about keeping secrets, and I wanted to give him the shortest possible window to sit with it. But that window kept getting smaller as I could never get him on the phone. It wasn't until we were about to leave town for the big night, disguised as a casual weekend getaway, when he finally called me back. June was only a few feet away and I didn't want to risk her seeing his name pop up on my phone, so as soon as he called, I scurried off out of our apartment. "I'm going to take a walk," I shouted behind me. It was odd timing as we had just packed our car and were ready to leave. But I didn't give her time to stop me.

While I knew that June didn't need me to ask her dad for permission, she would appreciate that I did it. Plus I wanted to. I'd always had a good relationship with John, but it was hard to find the perfect segue from small talk into marriage talk. At first I think he thought I was just giving him a report card about June: "She's an amazing person; we've had a great time together." But finally, I laid out my plan to him and ended with the question: "Can I ask your daughter to marry me?" There was a long pause—*oh boy*—then John told me to "hold on . . . I'm sorry, Paul. I left my phone in the store. Give me a second." I was so nervous, I agreed. "Sounds good." I listened to him go back into the store and speak to the person behind the register: "Did I leave my phone in here?" To which the cashier said, "Sir, you're holding it in your hand." Clearly, he was as nervous as I was.

He told me I didn't have to ask and of course he would grant his permission. Then he followed up: "When are you going to do it?" And I told him, "Later today." He wished me luck and I returned to the apartment to a confused June. "Where did you go?" I mumbled something and we went on our way. We arrived at a fancy beachside hotel, and I was nervous. I was going to ask her after dinner, so all I needed to do was just get through the next eight hours.

We placed our bags down in the room as I fake-casually said, "You know, I was thinking, after dinner we should go to this beach. It's supposedly amazing at night—the stars are incredible, and everyone makes their own bonfires. That would be fun, right?" I glanced at June out of the corner of my eye to see whether she expressed any suspicion or hesitation about my plan.

A moment passed, and she just looked at me and nodded nonchalantly. "Sure! Sounds fun."

I secretly clenched my fist in victory as I tried to retain my casual demeanor. "Oh, cool. I'll make sure I'm thinking of the right beach."

I pretended to search on my phone, and then as quickly as you could ask Jeeves, I announced, "Yup. That beach is real close." Then I repeated my question with a little unnecessary desperation, "So you want to go, right?"

June just repeated, "Yeah," while walking out to the balcony to take in the view. Stage 1 was complete. The plan was set.

We were at the hotel getting ready to go to dinner when I realized that I hadn't accounted for the ring box. Whenever you see someone in a movie present a ring, they seem to pull the box out of thin air. But I quickly learned that's *impossible to do*. These boxes are bulky as hell. I tried to jam the ring box in my pants, but the bulge looked ridiculous. I didn't know what to do. The easy answer would've been to lose the box. But years of movies and TV shows had led me to believe that the box was an essential part of the whole proposal. So now I was left with this problem: How could I keep this ring and ring box on me when it was warm as hell out and I had nowhere to hide it? I was starting to sweat. June was calling for me, and I needed more time, but I didn't want to give the illusion that I was having bathroom issues. So I hid the ring under the sink and exited, trying to act casual. June, of course, then went into the bathroom. *No!* I panicked. What if she found the ring?

I continued to play out a bunch of scenarios in my head about how I could hide the ring box, and it hit me just as we were leaving the room. I pretended I'd forgotten something, ran back into the room, and wrapped the ring box inside a sweatshirt. I reemerged, sweatshirt in hand, with a simple statement: "For the beach!" The idea was genius; not only did it hide the ring box, but it seemed natural and reiterated that we were going to a second location.

This perfect plan was busted when I realized I couldn't justify bringing the sweatshirt into the fancy restaurant. I'd have to leave it in the car, which meant I couldn't take any chances with a valet. So I did the most romantic thing possible and pulled into an open spot on the street near the restaurant. I really sold June on the money we were saving by self-parking instead of using the valet. By the time we got to the restaurant, I felt like I hadn't stopped sweating for an hour.

Despite the bumpy start, our dinner went really well, and soon it was time to go to the second location. My worst fears came to life when we got in the car and June said, "Do we have to?"

I had anticipated this question. This was why I was planting the seed and reconfirming the agreement to the second location throughout the day. If there was one thing I knew about June, it was that she was only capable of doing one planned event an evening. When June goes out at night, an unconscious internal timer in her head starts ticking. No matter what we are doing or how much fun we are having, if she if isn't in bed when the timer hits zero, it is not good. I love this about her. I know if she reads this, she will stop reading, put the book down, and say, "You are making me out to be a real beyach," but I truly love this quality of hers. I still don't understand all my own body's signals, so I am always impressed that she knows exactly how much energy she can expend in a day before she needs to reset.

June's internal timer influenced all our date nights. We never did dinner and a movie. It was dinner *or* a movie. I spend a lot of energy in our relationship doing mental Tetris, trying to fit multiple activities into a package that can be considered a single event. Thank

God for the Alamo Drafthouse, where we can have a drink at the bar, walk around the store, then head up to take in a movie and eat while watching it. That's *four* things in *one* location—a gold medal date night for us.

After many failed attempts to overschedule June, I've learned to respect her clock, so I rarely push back (she'd disagree), but tonight was one of those moments; I needed her to go. I don't remember exactly how I got her to agree—I think my brain was overloaded by stress at that point—but I'm sure some sort of bartering or pleading was involved.

When we finally made it to the beach, it was like a scene out of a movie: bonfires dotted the whole coastline, each surrounded by a different group of people playing football, drinking wine, or just staring quietly at the sky. As we walked along the shore, everything felt right, just like that night when we'd first kissed. I looked out for an empty spot and waited until we were alone to turn and face her.

I knelt down in front of her, and the nerves disappeared. I felt more confident than ever, looking up at this person I wanted to spend my entire life with. I didn't know what I was going to say; I had planned so much leading up to this moment that I had left this part a bit unscripted. "June, I am so happy I have found you. These last few years have been absolutely amazing . . ." As I went through some of the moments in our relationship, I realized once again what a great decision this was. I was pouring out my heart in a way I never had before but always wished I could, and then in a flourish I pulled the ring box from the rolled-up sweatshirt—success! I displayed the ring and said, "Will you marry me?"

"What the fuck are you talking about?!"

I scrambled to my feet and hid that ring on my person like I was a goddamn magician.

I didn't know what to do. This was all wrong. I had misjudged. She didn't feel the same way. I watched June's face change as she tried to make sense of what was actually happening. She sat down in the sand abruptly. I started to backpedal, but she cut me off.

"Is this a bit?" At this point, based on her reaction, for a split second I was going to say, "Yes!" That felt like it might be the best way out of this.

But then I realized, *Wait—she really does think this is some sort of bit!* I mean, I appreciated her faith in me as a comedian that she thought I could pull off such a dry and committed bit. I sat down next to her, and I said, "No, this isn't a bit. I just thought . . . you know . . . It's fine if you don't want to. I love you."

Her expression softened as she realized that the ring was real. The proposal was real. Everything was real. She started to cry and a huge smile burst across her face. *Okay, what's happening?* Was this a good thing or a bad thing? But before I could ask myself another five questions, she said, "Yes! Yes! Yes!"

At this point, I didn't even know what to do or how to feel. I'd experienced almost every human emotion in about forty-five seconds. I just said, "Really?" and as she nodded, I stood up and grabbed her by the hand as I pulled her in tightly for a kiss. This was the moment I had envisioned; we were kissing under a full moon on a beautiful night. We were engaged. Then, in the distance, I heard, *"Get a room!"*

We turned to see a twelve-year-old boy sitting alone on a bluff. He'd seen the whole thing. We turned and met his eyes. "I said get a room!"

It was actually good advice. The ride back to the hotel was full of tears and laughs, and as we excitedly entered the hotel, we announced to the night clerk, "We're engaged." She looked at us nonplussed. "So do you need something?" It hung in the air for a beat. "No . . . thank you." We went back to our room, sat on the bed for hours, and talked. I know she hates her reaction to my proposal and wishes we could redo that moment, but I wouldn't change it. Perfect isn't a thing. This night was uniquely us because of her reaction, and when I think back on this night, it always brings a smile to my face. It's got every piece of what I love about our relationship.

In the hotel room that night, we made a promise that, while I'd done this alone, from this day forward we'd do everything else together. And we have—unless it was an immersive theater experience.

BECOMING DAD

Our first son, Gus, was born on one of the busiest nights at Cedars-Sinai hospital. The energy in that place was like being at the hippest restaurant in town—they were overbooked, and they needed to flip tables. All the love, attention, and care we were given during childbirth became "You don't have to go home, but you can't stay here." We were thrust into the world and had to figure out how to take care of this new baby.

It's shocking how quickly your world changes when you have a kid. After that switch is thrown, everything moves fast. My baby was new to the world, and I was, too. I was in complete sensory overload. Those first few months are very emotional at all times on no sleep. I was in love with this new human in my life. I was overwhelmed by all these new responsibilities, I was exhausted, and I was mourning. I was mourning the death of my old life—which is a hard thing to admit, because I don't think you are supposed to be anything but happy about having a new baby and being a parent. And I was. But it's more complicated than that. You are transitioning from one chapter of your life to the next. June and I had kids in our thirties, and you forget how much freedom you take for granted by the time you get that old. You can pretty much go and do whatever, whenever you want. You can see late-night movies, have brunch with friends, make choices on a whim. But after you have a kid, the most mundane tasks become Herculean feats, and that is probably the toughest thing to get used to. Changing diapers is easy compared to running the simplest errand with a newborn.

One day, I made plans to take Gus to meet some friends at the park. While Gus napped, I showered (which went from being a daily thing pre-baby to something a little less predictable post-baby). When he woke up, I sprang into action. I changed him, dressed him, bundled him up, put him in his carrier, put a blanket over him, grabbed the diaper bag, folded up the stroller, put the stroller in the car, and put the carrier in the car. Ready to go.

Now I'm feeling accomplished, until a light pops on in the car: out of gas. *Shit. Okay, I can handle this*, I think, pulling into a gas station. I'm slightly worried as I ease the car next to the pump and turn it off, because maybe the lack of motion in the car will make Gus upset.

I quickly put my credit card in the reader. *Denied.*

Double shit.

The screen reads, "See cashier." The cashier is only ten feet away from the car. *Can I leave the baby in the car? I mean, I'm only going ten feet.* Suddenly, I remember a teacher from our baby class saying, "Never leave your baby in the car! If you leave your baby in the car, you could be arrested! They could take your baby away." So I stand frozen in the gas station lot, halfway between the car and the cashier like I'm in an invisible tug-of-war. I'm conflicted: *If the baby is within view, does it make a difference? Do feet matter? Fuck it.* I run back to the car, pop out the carrier, and carry the baby across the parking lot to the cashier, only to realize I have left my wallet in the car. So I head back to the car with the baby, grab my wallet, carry the baby back across the lot. Pay for the gas. Put the baby back in the car. Get back in the car and head to the park.

When I get to the park, I smell something from the back seat. *Okay, I know that smell. I gotta do a diaper change.* Because it's a park and there are no bathrooms nearby, I decide I'll change the baby in the car; I flip down the back seat and set up a little changing area. It's a little chilly, so I'm working fast to get him undressed while keeping him warm. With one hand, I wave a toy above him, and with the other, I'm doing cleanup, all while singing. When I remove the diaper, it's an explosion. Of course. I go to grab the baby wipes, and . . . nothing. I search the bag, but still nothing. There are no baby wipes. Now I have a naked baby and poop shrapnel is everywhere. What do I do?

I have an idea. I take off my sweatshirt, then the T-shirt underneath. I throw my sweatshirt back on, because a shirtless guy hanging around cars while dancing and singing with a toy in a public park is something you should call the cops about. I rip one of my favorite LA Clippers tees into a few strands (that was painful—I loved that shirt), grab water from Gus's bottle, wet the T-shirt strips, and create makeshift wipes. Genius! I get him in a new diaper, get him dressed, put him back in the carrier, pull the stroller out of the car, pop the stroller open, put the carrier in the stroller, grab the diaper bag, and meet up with my friend—only to realize I have five minutes before I have to leave and get back home for Gus's next nap. That was in many ways every day for the first year.

Your only true ally in this is your partner, and even that person can be hard to read. There was one night around 3:00 a.m. when June and I had been up and down the entire night. It was just another night in new baby hell, and she turned to me and said, "This sucks—I miss our old life." The biggest smile broke out across my face: "I do, too!" Then we burst out laughing, just giggling in a dark room, finally able to express the unspeakable. I don't think I've ever felt closer to another person. But also we knew what we meant; we loved our baby and didn't want to go back to our old life, we just wanted validation that this part sucked.

As I started to emerge from the haze of the baby years, I found a whole new set of problems arising, because whereas the baby used to be the issue, now it was all me. These thoughts started to creep in: *I'm a terrible dad . . . Ugh, I can't believe I let my baby look at a screen! . . . That dad is doing way cooler stuff with his kid than I am . . . Why don't I camp with my baby?* There is no end to this whirlwind of insecurity, and to make matters worse there is no total score to look at to see how you are doing in the international dad standings. No matter how well you think you might be doing, there is this voice in your head: *Are you doing enough?*

Every time I think I've figured something out, something new knocks me off balance. Like when my eight-year-old asked me whether Ja Morant was a bad guy because he was waving a gun in a crowded place (it's nuanced) or how to deal with the fear that my six-year-old, Sam, felt when he realized that I could die before him and made me promise I'd take him with me. Yes, I made a *Thelma & Louise* pact with my child, and I'm sure every parenting book would tell you not to. But it's done, and I stand by my decision.

I'm more than ten years into being a parent and new things keep popping up, and I'm still figuring it out. I make mistakes all the time, but I'm trying not to be so hard on myself anymore. I've learned that my job as a dad, besides being a joint protector, care-giver, and provider, is to be myself without judgment, flaws and all. I hope that my being myself lets my kids be themselves without feeling pressure to be anything but what they are. But if all else fails, no matter what I do or they do, I will support and love them. I don't think I knew just how strong that unconditional love was until I was on this side of it. My kids have made me a better person, be-cause I now bring this attitude into all of my relationships.

I love my parents, even though here I am writing a book in which I'm wrestling with how they raised me. The one thing I've never doubted is that they both love me and want to support me to the best of their abilities. I want my kids to feel the same way about me.

My new life feels like an eternal game of Tetris, but there is a freedom in knowing that no matter what you do, the bricks keep coming. Sometimes you sweep the board, and other times you get jammed in the corner; slowly but surely, you get back to an equilibrium. As long as you don't give up, you can stay in the game. I don't know whether that's exactly true for *Tetris*, but just go with me here, because my point is, I realized that *I love Tetris*. It's hard and at times frustrating, but the fulfillment you feel when you make a piece fit is worth it. And more often than not, when I look at my sons, I see the pieces slot into place.

ODE TO A MINIVAN

I'm not a car guy. I can't tell you what type of engine is in my car or . . . honestly, I don't even know enough about cars to make up a second thing that I don't know about them. My requirements for a car have always been pretty basic: Does it drive? If yes, then sold. Then, after Apple CarPlay came out, the question was twofold: Does it drive, and does it have Apple CarPlay? I'm a simple man, and that's all I cared about. I once didn't get a car that I really liked simply because it didn't have CarPlay.

My thinking changed when I had kids. Now my car has to accomplish a lot more. I basically need a U-Haul. I was nervous going on our first road trip with our newborn son, and I packed my tiny compact car completely full of literally every possible thing we'd ever need in case of an emergency, Uncle Buck style. I looked at the trunk and, in that moment, realized my life had forever changed. The contents of the trunk visually represented the physical and emotional weight I'd now be carrying as a parent. As I stood there taking it in, only then did I realize that there wasn't room for my own bags.

I thought we were prepared, but once we were on the road, we realized we had forgotten to pack the breast pump and baby bottles, but that's a whole different story—and for the benefit of our marriage, we decided that it was no one's fault. When we pulled up to the hotel valet, we needed three carts! That was a cart per person. June and I had only one bag each, and the baby was barely a person. How did we have so much stuff? But this was just the beginning. We regularly started traveling with forty to sixty pounds of *baby gear*. Then, after we had our second kid, there was even more gear, plus another car seat. Then, as soon as they grew out of that baby gear, we needed to start traveling with all of their other shit: bikes, scooters, balls, snacks.

At first, I was one of those parents who try to shove all this stuff into a regular car. I bent over deep at the waist to squeeze my kids into car seats that barely fit in the back of my car. It wasn't fun, but it was a battle I convinced myself I needed to wage in order to stay "cool"— because I was not getting a "family" car. Sure, I was a parent, but I was still cool, *goddammit*! I wasn't changing anything for my kids . . . except my entire life. Besides, what was I going to do, get a *minivan*!? *Haha, fuck no.* Life is too short. I'd rather throw out my back or travel without my own clothes to make extra room in the trunk than get a minivan. *No, no, no.* That suburban eyesore wasn't for me.

I'm here to tell you . . .

I was wrong!!!

Don't make the same mistake as me!

Get yourself a minivan!

Is this directed at new parents? Sure, I guess? But seriously, I think we should *all be driving minivans!*

Face it, your trunk sucks. Oh, but you have an SUV? That third row is great. *Go fuck yourself.* It's not. Those third rows are a joke. Show me a human leg that can fit in there comfortably up against that second-row seat back, which is way too close. You can't fit three people back there.

Get the minivan!

There seems to be this whole disinformation campaign about minivans: *Minivans suck.* Meanwhile, you're over here pretending your SUV isn't just a cop-out version of what I have. Bullshit, it is. Who are you trying to fool? Cheetos are on the floor, and Peppa Pig books are in all the back seat pockets. Get a minivan. Just own it.

Minivans made me a car guy. I remember the salesman was like, "You get this for your wife and you can get a cool car." And I was like, "You know what's cool? Not being an automotive misogynist! We buck gender norms in my household! Plus my wife won't drive it." But I don't care because this thing is all me. Yes, I've been known to take it on days when my wife has our kids, leaving her with her sleek sedan, because I want people to see me in my minivan.

I own it!

People might say (and they did say to me):

"I admire your courage."

"It takes big balls to drive that."

"Bet you can't wait till the kids are grown up."

To all of them I say: I have two kids, a wife, a ninety-pound dog, and relatives who love to visit with lots of luggage, and I carpool. Tell me what car can transport all that. Here's a hint: *none.*

None cars!!

To those of you who claim that the minivan is not sexy: Dare I say it? It's the sexiest car. First of all, Mark Wahlberg drives one—he's sexy, right? Plus how many sexy cars can fold all the seats down so you essentially have a king-size bed to have sex in? Not that fucking in your car should be a high priority. But it's an option available to the minivan driver.

Still don't believe me? Behold the power of what is possible with a minivan:

★ Control the weather with three different temperature zones in *one car.*

★ Twelve cupholders! Means each passenger can easily always have two drinks at their disposal at all times.

★ Have a family picnic . . . in the trunk.

★ Drive in the HOV lane without passengers, and no one will suspect a thing.

★ Three personal screens, each capable of playing its own entertainment, which means you can screen more films simultaneously than a small movie theater.

★ Never go hungry, as inevitably, someone has left some food in your car. All you have to do is find it. The game is afoot!

★ Sliding doors are cool as hell, and if they're operated correctly, you make it appear that you have a ghost chauffeur to open doors for you.

★ Three words: *Built-in. Vacuum. Cleaner.*

★ Help someone move . . . into a mansion.

★ Transport twenty-five rolled-up carpets on top of twenty-five rolled up carpets.

★ Prevents infidelity, as a minivan tells everyone that you're taken.

So I ask you to join me. Help me get this word out. This is my cause. Let's destigmatize Minivan Culture, because people have come to me who know my stance on the van, and they ask me in a hushed whisper, "Is it great?" And I say, "You have no idea."

So join me—get on board. There's always room for one more, and bring your beverages, too. And the best part? All of them have Apple CarPlay, and I'm sure it works with your fucking Android phone, too, and don't try to tell me an Android phone is better. I'll save that for another day.

WHAT'S YOUR PROBLEM

It was Father's Day 2021, and . . . do you remember the '90s movie *Fathers' Day* with Mel Gibson and Robin Williams? Wait, it wasn't Mel Gibson and Robin Williams; it was Robin Williams and Billy Crystal. No, I think Mel Gibson was in it—oh yeah, he was, but he just had a cameo, as a tattoo artist or something, or was that *The Hangover Part II*? Was he even in *Hangover II*, or was he just rumored to be in it? Was he a tattoo artist in both?

This is how my brain works. There is never a direct route to a point; it's a bunch of back roads and detours until, hopefully, I remember what I wanted to say, or better yet, I arrive at a new place that makes me forget that I ever wanted to say something. For 98 percent of my life, I chalked up this "energy" to being a creative New Yorker. Turns out it was a bit more complicated than that.

I thought I knew the entire story of me. There was one part, though, that I didn't really know until recently. But I'm getting ahead of myself, as usual.

"DoES HE HAVE AN oFF SWITCH?"

My childhood was filled with adults saying, "He's got a lot of energy!" "Does he have an off switch?" "He *really* likes to talk."

All kids have energy, but I had a bit more than most. I was "hyper." If you came over to my house, you were greeted at the door and given homemade tickets to a show starring me. Before you could even take off your jacket, you were whisked away to my room, where I'd rip those tickets, sit you down in a seat facing a makeshift stage, and then "perform." I eschewed traditional talent, like singing and dancing. That would require focus and practice, two things I didn't do. I just wanted to get right to the performing and accolades part. My shows always opened with a joke that I stole from late-night TV, like this David Letterman one: "Did you ever notice that on the back of garbage trucks, it says, 'Do not follow'? Well, if that's not just another case of meddling bureaucracy, I don't know what is." At the time, I didn't even know what the joke meant, but I felt that if I leaned into the intonation of the word *bureaucracy*, the joke might work. It didn't. But I was unfazed. I just segued into the main act, which was always a bit avant-garde, considering that I didn't have a traditional talent. I did stuff like pretending to shadowbox Mike Tyson (and lose), do an interpretative dance to the musical soundtrack of Robert Altman's *Popeye*, or perform ventriloquism, where I would prerecord the dummy's lines before the show. My shows had the energy of a community theater run by meth heads.

"CAN'T YOU JUST SIT STILL?"

My energy never ran out. If we went to the movies, we'd have to sit in the front row because I couldn't stay in my seat. I needed to jump up and "act" alongside the screen. So the idea of sitting down for something that wasn't as fun as a movie—such as dinner, school, church, or really anything—proved to be next to impossible. If I was forced to sit in one place for more than twenty minutes, my right leg would start bouncing up and down like I was performing a never-ending kick drum solo on an invisible bass drum. I couldn't help it; I had a compulsion to move my body.

"YOU NEED TO PAY MORE ATTENTION!"

When it came to school, even though I struggled to focus, I could always figure out a way to skate by. If the project was a book report, I'd ask the teacher whether I could come in as a character from the book instead and do a monologue about their life. Stuff like that always got me good grades and kept me from having to really do the nitty-gritty work of concentrating and writing long-form. Standardized tests were a different story. I didn't do well when it came to questions with black-and-white answers. These tests often revealed shocking disparities with my school grades. I was producing results coma patients might best. But it was also through these tests that I learned I was dyslexic. I worked hard at reading and even grew to love it. However, I'm still terrible at grammar, math, and science—basically anything that has "rules" or "correct answers." They're too confining for me.

"YOU LIKE EVERYTHING!"

In addition to being a ball of energy, I never ran out of things to talk about, because I liked everything. Scratch that; I *loved* everything, and I wanted to talk to whoever would listen about all these things in exacting detail, which led to many obsessions. Whenever I saw someone doing something that looked fun or cool, I'd want to do that, too, until I found the next thing that I wanted to devote my life to. This circle of life spun quickly, leaving in its wake acoustic guitars, magic sets, skateboards, Legos, basketball hoops, basketball cards, electric guitars, paints, small stuffed toy mice (don't ask), soccer balls, more magic sets, camping equipment, and even a racing bike. I was a Renaissance man without the patience to perfect (or, sometimes, even make passable) a single project.

"DON'T THINK."

Improv fit well with the way my brain worked. You say the first thing that comes into your head; you don't think. Finally, an art form that catered to my passion for lack of preparation.

The ability to make anything up, not have to remember it, and immediately move on to something else was perfect for my short attention span. And unlike my other hobbies, I never grew tired of improv. But improv wasn't a magic pill.

"YOU HAVE A PROBLEM."

Throughout my life, I'd noticed that I had some odd quirks: I could get to a place early and somehow get distracted and arrive fifteen minutes late; I'd just blurt out things I knew I shouldn't say; I'd go into obsessive rabbit holes that took over all my concentration, from Wikipedia deep dives to needing to clean my entire apartment before I could sit down to do the work I actually needed to get done. I never thought to ask why I would always wait until the last minute to do something I had to do—including *big* things, like writing my wedding vows. I loved that high of finishing something just under the wire. When confronted with any of these issues by a friend or girlfriend, I turned it back on them for not "getting me." I didn't have a problem; they did, or so I thought.

* * *

Wait, where was I? Father's Day 2021 (see, I knew I'd finally get back to the point of this story): During one of those moments when I should have been enjoying my breakfast in bed and just relaxing, I started scrolling Twitter—a place where I used to find myself oddly more confrontational than in any other area of my life, and over the stupidest of stuff. Mainly shutting down haters and championing my favorite NBA team, the LA Clippers. Within minutes I got into a Twitter feud with a Clippers hater that I just couldn't let go. It wasn't a vulgar exchange; I was just picking apart the words in each tweet he sent me. After a few back-and-forths, the hater responded with a tweet that changed everything: "You are hyperfixating. I have ADHD, and I think you have ADHD, too. You should check that out!"

While this was not a traditional insult or a slam, it was a diagnosis leveled with such bluntness that it rattled me for a good minute. I then responded by sending him a short video of Martin Lawrence in concert, not the one I saw with my dad, grabbing his nuts and saying, "You wanna criticize something, criticize these nuts!" (Thanks to the hilarious Chelsea Peretti for uploading that clip for us all to use.)

While I felt good shutting that guy down, I couldn't get his comment out of my head. Did I have ADHD? Now, having read this far, you may be thinking, *How did you not realize this earlier?* But truly, it never crossed my mind. I get shit done. I pay my bills. I can memorize my lines, and I can keep a job. I don't have a problem. That's not me. I decided to prove to myself that this guy was wrong. So I started looking at ADHD Twitter accounts. As I started reading through posts on the topic, there were some interesting articulations of things that I totally identified with: some major, such as the way a small rejection could spiral me into a dark mood; some minor, like the way I tend to buy too many notebooks and use each one only until about a quarter of the pages are filled, which I learned is a "manifestation of novelty seeking, perfectionism, and boredom, on repeat."

At first, these testimonials from people who struggled with ADHD seemed to make for interesting coincidences, but then I kept scrolling. It was as though I was being seen for the first time; I couldn't believe it. After scrolling for about thirty minutes, the appropriate amount of internet time to diagnose myself, I was convinced. I had ADHD. When June walked in to check on me, I exclaimed, "I think I have ADHD!" She barely looked up and said, "Oh yeah, of course you do."

She was so nonchalant and confident, just like the Twitter hater, that once again, I was shook. I felt like I was totally in the dark.

How had I not known? I was in the final scene of a murder mystery, actively trying to find the killer, and realizing it was me. I started thinking back to these moments in my life, these quotes I had heard variations of since I was a child. In a fit of anger, a friend had once said to me, "Not everyone's brain works like yours." When I heard that, I thought he was apologizing for not being able to keep up with how I did things, but I now realized that the meaning was precisely the opposite. I expected people to mirror my way of doing things and always felt let down when they couldn't keep up—but I was the weird one.

So I took the next logical step: I spoke to my therapist. She recommended a few books, which I devoured in one sitting. What did you expect? I'm compulsive. Everything was coming into focus. It was like finding the guidebook of my life laid out in front of me. The things I had never dared articulate about how I felt weren't to be feared or shunned; they were indicative of something bigger, and maybe something I could fix.

I then saw a psychiatrist who officially diagnosed me with ADHD. She wanted to prescribe something, but my first instinct was *hell no*.

I wanted to fix myself, but taking a pill felt like I was admitting defeat. It was an ambivalent feeling: wanting help but not taking it because it made me feel like I needed help—a feeling that I still wrestled with from my youth. Plus, what if I didn't like the me I was on the medication. I had gotten this far in my life without it, and I didn't want to mess that up. The psychiatrist eased me into taking a pill. She put me on the lowest dose; she assured me I could stop this medication without experiencing the side effects that are common with some other brands. So I started taking the medication. The change was instantaneous. The world came into focus, or better, I could focus without dealing with the whole world around me. Having blinders on is usually a way to describe a limited worldview, but that is how this pill made me feel—and it was a relief. I could sit longer, wait my turn, and focus on one thing and not want to do something else after ten minutes. I still had instincts that might briefly pull me into my old traps, but I'd always quickly re-center.

The other thing I realized after taking the pill for a month or so was the lack of stress I felt. I wasn't overwhelmed by my choices. I just enjoyed what I was doing when I was doing it. Then, as things were settling into a new normal, I took the natural next step: I stopped taking the pills. I couldn't kick this feeling that I was a failure if I couldn't fix myself with sheer willpower. However, being off the meds just amplified all the feelings and behaviors I had before I started taking the pill, because now I knew the difference. My ADHD felt worse than ever. I missed the sense of relief I felt on the pill. Why would I deny myself that? The only person it hurt was me. So I pushed my ego to the side and let this pill do it's job. I went back on the medication, and I haven't looked back.

I don't usually talk about my struggle with ADHD. Fewer than ten people in my life know about it, and I told most of them only after they had told me that they suffered from it, too. Talking about it often embarrasses me: even the phrase I just wrote, "my struggle with ADHD," reads like the headline of a bad celebrity article in a glossy magazine. So I keep it on the DL. Why share it now? Because I realized that if it weren't for people on Twitter sharing their experience, I wouldn't have taken the first step to do something that changed my life. If I had had access to that earlier or a way to see ADHD as different from just being "hyper," maybe I could have taken some steps toward positive change. And maybe someone reading this chapter will have a realization, too.

There is one thing I know for sure: it's never too late to make a change. Also, Mel Gibson wasn't in *The Hangover Part II*. He was supposed to have been a tattoo artist, but then the cast and crew boycotted, so his part was scrapped. And in *Fathers' Day*, he was Scott, the body piercer. Which was pretty funny if I'm remembering it correctly, I think.

MY WING WOMAN

I'm lucky to have a partner who is my best friend. We are a team, forever tied together as the protectors of our amazing kids and to each other as our number one ride-or-die supporters. But the actual test of any couple is how the two of them react in a crisis.

We are always running each other through the darkest scenarios and mentally role-playing what we'd do.

What is the escape plan in case of a fire?

How would you fend off rabid coyotes?

If a crazy trio of invaders broke into our house, the way they did in that M. Night Shyamalan movie with Dave Bautista, and told us we have to kill one of us for the rest of the world to live, what would you do?

Thankfully, most of these moments haven't occurred, at least not yet, although I did see Dave Bautista once and got very scared.

No matter how much we prep, we are continually tested by circumstances we have never imagined. A few weeks after our first child was born, June and I were fried. We were working nonstop in service to our leader, a baby. We buzzed around him like he was a Hollywood star with Mariah Carey–level demands. (He insisted on milk at exactly 98.5 degrees, only wore white onesies, and needed a Diaper Genie in every room.) We were overworked and exhausted, on a work shift that never ended. Even though we had not left each other's side for more than a few minutes in those weeks, we felt like coworkers instead of a couple—just tag teaming in and out to give each other a few moments of rest. Our friends urged us to take a break, walk, get a drink—do something to feel like humans again. So we did. We took showers, dressed in something other than comfy cozies, left the baby at home with my friends, and went out into the world.

A new bar had opened in our hood. It was a hip place with plenty of exposed wood beams and strategically placed industrial machinery now designated as art. It catered to a crowd of people who did not have a care in the world—basically us nine months ago. Everything seemed so crowded and loud. Were bars always this way?

We found a seat at the bar and ordered a drink. That felt like a huge accomplishment, just to be somewhere other than home, and it felt good. We had done it. We left the house. It was just the two of us. It was perfect. Then suddenly, we heard in a thunderously booming voice, "*Get the fuck out of my seat!*"

I turned around and saw a guy approaching who was the epitome of a hipster douche. He had tight pants, tousled hair, a deep

V-neck tee, and an extra-long chunky scarf around his neck. Before I could even reply, he yelled again, "*I said, get that cunt out of my seat!*"

You don't talk to my wife this way. I felt that old Hulk energy rise to the surface. I turned to him, looked him dead in the eyes, and said, "Um. Excuse me?"

Okay, not the strongest comeback. I was a bit rusty in the confrontation/anger department—see, therapy did help. Also, to be fair my tone was pretty harsh. Plus it was deafening in there, and I did want to get some clarity before I fully engaged.

Without missing a beat, he walked closer and repeated himself. "I said, get your dumb bitch out of my chair." Now we were nose to nose, and I guess I had heard him correctly, after all. So the gloves were coming off.

As an actor, writer, and comedian, I can think on my feet and unleash a devastating barb at a moment's notice. That's why I looked at him and said . . .

"Oh yeah?"

Wait! What? That was the best I could come up with? I could have said, "Lenny Kravitz called. He wants his scarf back" or "Did it hurt when you came in last place in a Wilmer Valderrama look-alike contest?"

But no, I said, "Oh yeah?" with the energy of someone who had just dropped the mic in a rap battle.

Unfazed by my cutting slam, this hipster upped the ante and said, "You better move before I kick a watermelon seed through your front teeth."

Yes, I'm a gap-toothed man, and this use of vivid imagery created a lovely and, more important, unexpected image that connoted a much more whimsical tableau than the aggressive vibes coming at me. So, point to the hipster. As a matter of fact, if you are keeping track, I was losing this verbal battle. I needed to come back hard. I wasn't going to let what had just happened happen again. Oh no, now I was ready. So I looked this guy dead in the eyes, and I blurted out, "I bet you'd want to put my dick in between my front teeth!"

Internally, I yelled, *What?! What the hell does that even mean?!* Then something unexpected happened. He responded with, "Yeah, I do!"

This took me entirely off guard. I responded, "You do?!"

Inadvertently, I had just made this guy question his entire vision of his own heteronormative masculinity, a trick the WWE has been using for years. Now he was confused and angry. He cocked back his fist. Everything went silent.

Then, all of a sudden, an open hand came flying into my field of vision and smacked this dude across the face so hard.

Swack!

The entire bar audibly gasped.

Was that my hand? No, it couldn't be; I haven't moved. It was June! Acting on this moment of masculine confusion, she had let one loose and slapped this guy silly.

There is nothing more insulting than a smack across the face. It's humiliating. When you smack someone across the face, you are signaling *I don't even care enough to hit you—I just want to embarrass you.*

When the hipster turned back to us, recovering from the flesh-on-flesh trauma, he sported a perfectly formed red handprint across his face. He looked shocked; we stood there for a moment in stunned silence. Then, without warning, he took off. He ran out of the bar like a deflated high school bully from an '80s movie.

We had just been in a bar fight, a scenario we had never discussed or prepped for, and we had won! We had defeated the aggro hipster. The bar cheered. The bartender bought us drinks, and we felt we were on top of the world. It was time to celebrate. A few moments later, a waitress approached us and casually mentioned that the guy June slapped had just gotten out of jail and could be "dangerous."

What now?!

The record scratched on our internal victory song, and reality suddenly set in. *We don't need to mess with a convict; we're parents now.* We slammed back our drinks, left a tip on the bar, and got the hell out of there. As a matter of fact, we've never been back to that bar. Not worth it.

We arrived back home refreshed and happy and stronger than ever. As we go forward in this life together as a couple and a family, we will never know what's coming our way. But I genuinely believe that we'll be able to handle it as long as I provide enough of a distraction for my wife to land a perfect sucker punch.

EPILOGUE

A.K.A. WRAP IT UP . . .

I guess this is the big end moment when I tell you, "This is me. I've grown, I've changed, I've learned, and most important, please buy my nutritional supplements." (*Note to self:* Start selling nutritional supplements.) But that would be a lie. This is just a small part of me, a snapshot of some moments in my life. It's just the contents of a few of my boxes. It's not the full story—unless this book doesn't sell. Then, this might be the definitive recollection of my life. (*Reminder to editor:* Revisit this line for the paperback edition after I see the sales numbers.)

I'm still a work in progress, and I'm not afraid to admit that I don't know what's next and I haven't fully figured everything out. But I do know that every time I've opened myself up to others (even when I was just telling a funny story)—revealing a fear, an insecurity, or an embarrassing moment—it has not only made me stronger but it also connected me to those around me so much more. I wish I hadn't spent so much time pretending to be someone I wasn't just to make others happy or equating vulnerability with weakness. These were survival mechanisms, and as much as I regret that, I'm thankful I'm getting a chance to course correct. I take pride in every turn I take that's different from what was laid out in front of me as a child. But I also embrace everything, good and bad, that made me who I am. This is why I'm able to have joyful recollections of trauma.

And don't worry, I have more stories to tell—more trauma to unpack. I mean, I didn't even mention the time I did a movie with Nicolas Cage . . .

HOW DID THIS GET MADE!?

Writing a book is a marathon, and while there were countless hours alone hunched over a keyboard, there were so many amazing people supporting me along the way.

I don't think I could have tackled this project if I didn't have my incredibly talented and funny assistant, Molly Reynolds, at my side. She read everything, from embryonic first drafts to final edits, before anyone else, and her reaction to these pieces many times gave me the encouragement to keep going. Together we have wrestled with countless Google Docs and have lost many battles with Microsoft Word, and I couldn't think of a better partner in this process and in everything I do. Thank you.

The reason why you are reading this is simply due to the time that my agents at Aevitas took with me when this project was in its infancy. David Kuhn and Nate Muscato guided me through every step of the process from pitch to production. They stood by me whenever I had a question or grievance, or just needed to vent. Their sound advice was always spot on. The note to "go deeper" was one that rung true from the first meeting till they pried this manuscript out of my hands.

A special thanks to Katy Hamilton, my first editor, who championed this project and believed in me and knew what this book could be. Rakesh Satyal came in less than two weeks before the manuscript had to go to my copyeditor and rolled up his sleeves and dove in headfirst. Within days it was like he had been there the entire time, and I'm thankful he's been behind me ever since.

I'm incredibly lucky for the entire team at Harper: Ryan Amato, Ann Edwards, Courtney Nobile, Sarah Schoof, and Nina Gomez. Their knowledge, support, and excitement has kept me afloat and inspired me since our first Zoom meetings. A huge shout-out to Cathy Cambron and Crissie Molina, who grammatically wrestled this beast and tamed its syntactical inconsistencies and helped streamline some of my more complicated thoughts. As well as my top-notch audiobook team of Abigail Nover and Nathan Rosborough, who helped bring this book to life in an entirely unique way. You should check it out.

Laura Kindred, thank you for being my eyes when I needed them the most. This book is better because of you.

I love telling stories, and when they came out on episodes of How Did This Get Made?, I never imagined the reaction to them would be so strong. *HDTGM* listeners, this book is for you. But instead of thank you I will simply say, GEOOOSTOORM!!

I consider myself very lucky to have told these stories, many for the first time, to my OG editors, Jason Mantzoukas and June Diane Raphael. I love doing *HDTGM* with you, and I can't imagine better partners. Your piercing questions and hilarious commentary on my childhood stories made me realize that maybe my normal childhood wasn't that normal after all. However, you are totally wrong about #TeamFred.

I'm forever grateful to my *How Did This Get Made?* team. Over the past fourteen years many have come and gone, and each of you left your indelible mark on the development of this show with your talent and patience, including but not limited to Colin Anderson, Scott Auckerman, Mike Berkowitz, Devon Bryant, Jess Cisneros, Rich Garcia, Avaryl Halley, Casey Holford, Adam Sachs, Scott Sonne, Jeff Ullrich, and Kyle Waldron. A special thanks to Codi Fischer, who set a new standard for the show and has remained an ever-present watchful eye over it ever since.

While we are talking about podcasts, I must thank Marc Maron; when I appeared on his show, I started talking about my story in a way I never had. It was the first step in my journey to go a little deeper, and the DNA of that conversation is all over this book. Same for Seth Rogen. When I was compiling stories to tell on his podcast, it was the first time that I felt like: *Oh, there is so much here I've never shared; I think I have a book here.*

Everyone should have a friend like Sam Srinivasan, who is smart, savvy, fun, and always there to support. She's always in my corner, and her help is invaluable in so many ways I can't even begin to list them. She was also the first person to get me to write long-form, and that reignited my passion for writing after writing so many social media short bursts.

One of the most important things you need to write a book is time. I'm very lucky to have a person in my life that affords me that time. Juliana De La Torre watches over our children and helps our family in countless ways. I'm forever grateful for finding you and the time you have given our family.

There are so many people that have been sounding boards and advice givers and just simply inspirations as I've tackled this project.

Casey Wilson, your writing is inspired, and you gave me such great advice in every step of this process.

Robyn E. Smith, this book is an outgrowth of the work we have done, and I'm forever grateful that I was able to have you on this journey with me.

Justin Halpern, thank you for support, advice, and wisdom. If I get to sign books at Costco, it's because of you. Your books are hilarious and inspirational, and Go Strom!

Kate Black, your recon gave me relief.

Matt Labuguen, you have a magic touch; thank you for sharing it with me.

Grant Dziak and Celeste Bonin, you expanded me.

Owen Burke, you were the first person to buy this book at FULL PRICE, and that articulates everything I love about you. You epitomize always getting your friends' backs.

Flanny, in addition to being a great friend, you gave me a show and pushed me to tell stories. I would have never done that without your unwavering support.

Rob Huebel, a lot of people know you for your luscious lips and sexy gaze, but what people don't know is how supportive you are as a friend, and it means the world to me.

The Hanging with Paul Scheer Discord, 3 Things Substack, and Thursdays with Paul and Rob regulars. Chatting with you is always a highlight of my week.

Shawna Wexler, I love having you on my team.

Max Nagler, thanks for chasing big ideas.

All the assistants at Aevitas, UTA, Verve, WME, Sechel PR, and Sugar 23. We all know you make this world run.

David Caspe, Mike Daniels, Marcelle Karp, Michaela McManus, Amy Nicholson, Josh Richmond, and Amanda Schweizer for your friendship.

Largo, UCB Theater, Dynasty Typewriter, the Elysian, and Chicago City Limits, these are some of the best places to see live comedy and improv. Thank you for always having a place for me on your stages.

I talk a lot about the crew of people that have my back throughout this book, but I don't call them out by name. I'm so lucky I've gotten to perform on those stages with Owen Burke, Nicole Byer, Chad Carter, Jackie Clarke, Lisa Gilroy, Mary Holland, Rob Huebel, Brian Huskey, Phil Augusta Jackson, Nick Kroll, Jason Mantzoukas, Jack McBrayer, Seth Morris, Dannah Phirman, Rob Riggle, Charlie Sanders, Danielle Schneider, Jessica St. Clair, and Carl Tart. I consider you all my second family.

Oh, and of course, my third family, Steve Ballmer, Ty Lue, and the entire LA Clippers organization—you make it all worthwhile.

One of my biggest thank-yous must go to, my parents, Bill Scheer and Gail Donheiser, I love you both very much. I hope that in telling these stories that comes through.

I'm forever grateful to my entire family—the ones I've known since birth and the ones I've gained along the way. I have always wanted brothers and new sisters, and I have them now—Deanna and Wing Cheng, Gina and Frank Pantina, and Lauren and Al Persico.

Christine Scheer, for what you have added to my dad's life and mine.

My only regret is that John and Diane Raphael and Walter Donheiser weren't alive to read this.

Gus and Sam, my two guys, every day is sweeter with you two in it. My love for you knows no bounds. I'm proud of everything you do and who you are. You make every day better, funnier, and sweeter. I love watching you grow.

And while I know I've sung her praises a bunch of times throughout this book, I simply must do it again. June is my rock. I could write another book about how she helped me with this one. In writing this, I always had you in my mind reading it, and to hear your laughter when you read it was really the only thing I needed. I love you. You are the hottest woman alive and I never have seen anyone as beautiful as you.

But I also want to thank you! You actually bought the book—that's huge. Most of these other people I thanked got it for free. But since I don't know you, I'll let you fill this in yourself.

Finally and most importantly, I have to thank _____.

(name)

They have always been such a big supporter of me and my work. I remember when I told them I was writing this book, they told me the best piece of advice, they said, "Paul, _____

_____

(piece of advice)

_____."

And that's how this book got made; it's because of everyone I just mentioned. I'm forever grateful.

ABOUT THE AUTHOR

Paul Scheer is a comedian, Screen Actors Guild Award–winning actor, filmmaker, and podcaster known for his numerous roles in film and television, including on *Black Monday*, *30 Rock*, *Fresh Off the Boat*, *Veep*, and *The League*. He also cocreated and starred in *Human Giant* and *NTSF:SD:SUV::*. Paul cohosts the podcast *How Did This Get Made?* with actors June Diane Raphael and Jason Mantzoukas, as well as the *Unspooled* podcast with film critic Amy Nicholson. He lives in Los Angeles with his wife, June, and his sons, Gus and Sam. Paul performs regularly at Largo in Los Angeles and around the country with *How Did This Get Made?* and Dinosaur. Go LA Clippers and go to www.paulscheer.com for more info.